POLAND

STEVEN OTFINOSKI

☑® Facts On File, Inc.

AN INFOBASE HOLDINGS COMPANY

Poland

Facts On File, Inc.
11 Penn Plaza
New York, NY 10001

Library of Congress Cataloging-in-Publication Data

Otfinoski, Steven.
    Poland / Steven Otfinoski.
        p.   cm. — (Nations in transition)
    Includes bibliographical references and index.
Summary: Examines the history, politics, and culture of Poland,
    with an emphasis on its transition from a communist to a free nation.
        ISBN 0-8160-3063-4
        1. Poland—History—1980–1989.   2. Poland—History—1989–
    [1. Poland.]   I. Title.   II. Series.
    DK4442.088   1995
    943.805'6—dc20   95-17252

Facts On File books are available at special discounts when purchased in bulk quantities for businesses, associations, institutions, or sales promotions. Please contact our Special Sales Department in New York at 212/967-8800 or 800/322-8755.

Text design by Catherine Rincon Hyman
Cover design by Nora Wertz

MP FOF 10 9 8 7 6 5 4 3 2 1

This book is printed on acid-free paper.

*T*o Agnes and Jacob,

my grandparents

Contents

A Personal Preface

*H*er name was Agnes. She came from Tarnów in southwestern Poland, a place that had supported her forefathers for generations. But in the early years of the 20th century, it was no longer a place where she felt she had a future. So, at the age of 18, Agnes left her homeland with a group of friends and relatives and sailed on a passenger ship to America—a land of opportunity for millions of immigrants from Europe.

She settled in New England, in the state of Connecticut. Here, she fell in love with another Polish immigrant, a meat cutter. They married, had a child, and life was good, until one day tragedy struck. Agnes's husband died of tuberculosis. Alone and without friends in a strange land, Agnes returned to Poland with her small son, but not for long. A short time later, she decided to return, convinced she could still find happiness in the United States.

She and her son settled again in Connecticut in the tiny community of Rockfall, where she found work and a room in a boardinghouse that catered to Polish immigrants. It wasn't long before her son caught pneumonia and died. Soon after this, she met another Pole, an ambitious young man named Jacob. They fell in love and married. After suffering an industrial accident that left him blind in one eye, Jacob used the compensation money to buy some farmland in nearby Middletown. Here the couple established a farm, which they worked with their seven children—six boys and a girl. (An eighth child died in a kitchen accident.)

Agnes and Jacob Otfinoski were not extraordinary people. Their hardships and tragedies were shared by millions of immigrants. Yet their story is important to me because they were my grandparents.

The Poland of the grand cities of Warsaw and Kraków and their thousand-year-old culture was not the Poland they had known. Their Poland was a much grimmer place, of overcrowded urban slums and rural areas devastated by famine and the dislocation of war. It was such conditions that drove them and thousands of other working-class Poles to leave their homeland and come to America to find a better life. There they pursued the same trades—farming, mining, manual labor—they had known in Poland. For many of them, their lives became far better than what they had been back home. And their hard work and perseverance promised an even better life for their children.

My Polish heritage was not an important part of my childhood. Unlike my cousins, I did not attend St. Mary's parochial school, where religion and Polish were required subjects. My father, the next to the youngest child, was the only one who moved away from the family homestead after his service in World War II (although he later moved back) and married my mother, a German-American girl, from New York City. My father does not even speak very good Polish. When he talked it around the rest of the family, so the story goes, they would laugh at him.

What I do remember from my childhood are the hearty holiday meals we shared in my grandmother's tiny kitchen on Christmas Eve and Easter. Every Easter, the centerpiece on the dinner table would be a beautifully sculptured lamb made of butter. It was a gift from the good sisters of St. Mary's, the local Polish Catholic church my grandparents helped found.

My grandparents did not instill a strong sense of what it was to be Polish in their children and grandchildren, except by their example. Until the day she died, my grandmother was a devout Catholic, a warm, loving person, and as humble and simple as the Polish soil from whence she came. My grandfather was more distant, but in his younger days, he had been a colorful character—hard-working, hard-drinking, and as ambitious to get ahead as any immigrant. He learned how to give haircuts by watching the barber down on Main Street, sold dry goods and homemade whiskey in a general store he ran, and raised horses that he raced on weekends with his Polish friends.

For all that happened to them in their new homeland, my grandparents never forgot they were Poles and they never forgot Poland.

Today, the Poles have little reason to want to leave their beloved homeland. With the collapse of communism in 1989 and the establishment of a democratic political system and a free-market economy, Poland, like most of Eastern Europe, has become a nation of renewed spirit and hope. But as Poland makes the transition from communism to democracy, new problems and challenges have arisen. This book will examine these challenges as seen through the prism of Poland's past, its land, people, culture, and religion.

1

An Introduction to the Land and Its People

It has been said that in the world's history, geography determines destiny. The United States—separated from Europe and Asia by two mighty oceans and graced with a temperate climate, abundant natural resources, and peaceful nonthreatening neighbors to the north and south—has developed into one of the world's mightiest superpowers. Few countries on earth have been so blessed with good geography as the United States. Few countries have been as poorly served by geography as Poland.

Located in the heart of Europe, Poland is mostly a flat, fertile plain with no mountains, rivers, or other natural obstacles to the west or east to protect it from its powerful neighbors—Germany to the west and Russia to the east. In its thousand-year history, Poland has been the victim of countless invasions, not just from these two nations, but from the Mongols to the east, the Swedes to the north, and the Turks and Czechs to the south.

But Poland has not always been so vulnerable. There was a time, between invasions and defeat, when Poland was one of the most powerful nations in Europe. Since that "golden age," however, Poland has been conquered, divided, partitioned, and finally gobbled up by its greedy neighbors so that it no longer existed as an independent country.

This curse of geography may be expected to have produced a people who are weak, vacillating, and cowardly. But the Poles are a strong, proud people with a rich and age-old culture. The blows that fate has dealt them over the centuries has ennobled their character, made them resilient, enduring, and resourceful. Their very lack of freedom has made the Poles cling all the more fiercely to the ideal of freedom and its fruits. Few nationalities are more deserving of the name "freedom fighters" than the Polish people. Deprived of their very country for over a century, they kept it alive in their hearts. Through pogroms, repressions, failed rebellions, and the threat of total extinction in the 20th century, Poles kept hope alive as expressed in the opening words of their national anthem:

> Poland has not perished yet
> So long as we still live.[1]

But there is also a dark side to this national character. Poland's love of freedom has, in the past, paradoxically been the very instrument by which the nation has lost it. Dissent and disagreement have led to internal conflict and political chaos, further aggravated by a long tradition of self-interest among the highborn and wealthy. For centuries, the Polish nobility refused to give up their power for national unity and the good of the country. Romantic and idealistic in their quest for independence, Poles have historically failed time and again to turn those ideals into political realities. As novelist James Michener has written, "Personal freedom was the lifeblood of Poland but the supreme irony was that its freedom-loving

The serene beauty of Poland's Lakes Region is captured in this picture of Suwalki, in the country's northeast corner. (Polish National Tourist Office, New York)

citizens were not able to develop those governmental forms which would preserve that freedom."[2]

Like so many of the great nations of the world, Poland is a mass of contradictions—a freedom-loving people too often ill-equipped to handle freedom, a downtrodden country that has never given up hope, a land of a devoutly religious people who lived for 40 years under the atheistic regime of communism. To understand Poland better, it is necessary to look closely at the land itself, its people, resources, and geographical regions. Although dominated by flat plains, on a closer look, Poland is surprisingly diversified geographically.

The Seven Geographical Regions

Poland is the second largest country in Eastern Europe. Only Russia is bigger. Its landmass, enlarged and shrunken by countless wars and border disputes, is presently 120,725 square miles (312,678 km), roughly the size of the British Isles or the state of New Mexico.

Poland is bordered on the north by the Baltic Sea, beyond which lies Sweden. To the south, are the rugged Carpathian Mountains and the Czech Republic and Slovakia. To the west is Germany and to the east, Russia.

From north to south, Poland has seven distinct regions. Along the Baltic coast, Poland's only access to the sea, is a narrow strip of sun-filled beaches and pleasant resorts that is called the "Polish Riviera." On either end of this sandy stretch are two natural harbors, home to the important port cities of Szczecin and Gdansk. The workers of Gdansk are an independent and defiant breed, and Polish freedom was reborn through their efforts in the 1980s under the banner of the Solidarity movement.

Below the coastal lowlands is a broader swath of land known as the Lakes Region. Foreigners surprised to find Poland has a Riviera, may be equally surprised to discover this wooded region dotted with 7,703 lakes. Formed largely by prehistoric glaciers, many of these small lakes are joined by rivers and canals, allowing vacationers to sail or canoe along the pristine waterways for many miles. The Lakes Region's primary industry is tourism. The Poles who live here are proud of the natural beauty of their land and are eager to share it with visitors. Their hospitality, something a tourist experiences everywhere in Poland, is best expressed by the old Polish proverb, "A guest in the home, God in the home."[3]

The forests and lakes teem with wildlife, including swans and cranes and the largest herd of elk found in Europe. Lumbering is also important, although farming is limited mostly to rye and potatoes.

Below the Lakes Region are the Central Plains, the heart of Poland. Long the stomping grounds of Poland's enemies, this flat, green plain is covered by thousands of farms and the great Polish cities of Poznan, Wroclaw, Lódz, and Warsaw, the capital. The reawakening of life, often grim under communism, can perhaps best be seen in one of the region's poorer cities, such as Bialystok, which lies northeast of Warsaw. New construction and freshly painted buildings are brightening the once gray urban landscape. "Look around," Deputy Mayor Ewa Bonczak-Kuytcharczyk told a foreign reporter. "This place is booming with construction." But her pride is mixed with scorn for the new government that is responsible for the changes. "The Democratic Left Alliance [made up of mostly former Communists] is rather better at spending money than investing."[4]

Life has changed less for the farming families in the countryside. They continue to work the hard soil, less fertile than in other regions, to make it produce sugar beets, rye, potatoes, and other crops.

The region is transversed by Poland's two great river systems: the Bug-Vistula-Notec-Worta system and the Oder-Worta and Odra system. The Vistula is the country's single longest river, rising in the Carpathian Mountains in the south, flowing across the plains and emptying into the Baltic Sea, 675 miles (1,086 km) away from its source.

Among the natural preserves located in this region is Bialowieza National Park, whose 312,000 acres (125,000 hectares) straddle Poland and Russia. A national park since 1919, Bialowieza is Europe's only remaining primeval forest and home to the largest herd of bison in the world. The story of Poland's bison illustrates a resiliency that matches that of its people.

Once protected by Polish royalty in their hunting grounds, the bison dwindled in recent centuries and were completely killed off and eaten by starving soldiers in World War I. In 1929, three pairs of native bison were brought in from European zoos and returned to their natural habitat. They multiplied and numbered 250 by the mid-1980s. The Poles have since returned the favor and now send their bison to zoos and preserves across the globe to start new herds.

Just south of the plains are the Polish Uplands, consisting of rolling hills and lofty mountains. This well-populated area is rich in fertile farmland and mineral deposits. Uplands farms are found mostly in the east and produce wheat, corn, and potatoes. The region around the city of Katowice contains one of the world's largest coalfields, where generations of Polish workers have gone down into the mines for a living. Coal is Poland's most precious natural resource, and it is the world's sixth largest producer of coal. Other minerals found in the Uplands include copper, lead, and zinc, while the city of Oppela is famous for its cement industry.

South of the Uplands is a narrow belt known as the Carpathian Forelands. The region's fertile soil supports many farms and a dense population. Its major city is the ancient and venerable Kraków, home to

Poland's oldest university. Outside Kraków is Nowa Huta, center of Poland's steel and iron industries.

Forming Poland's southern border is the Western Carpathian Mountains district. Their tallest peak, Rysy, rises to over 8,000 feet (2,499 m), the nation's highest point above sea level. A popular vacation spot, the Carpathians are thick with forests and include several national parks. The Highlanders who live here are a hardy, independent people instantly identifiable by their colorful folk costumes and the *ciupagi*, a mountaineer's cane with an ax handle, they carry. Their traditional homes, made of mountain timber, are as unique as they are.

Tucked away in the southwest corner of Poland is the seventh geographical region, the Sudetes Mountains. These lower peaks rise to under 5,000 feet (1,500 m) above sea level and are older than the Carpathians. The cities and towns of this region are home to a thriving textile industry.

The Polish climate varies from region to region but is generally milder at the coast than inland and colder in the mountains than the plains and lowlands. January temperatures average 26° F (–30° C) and 73° F (23° C) in July.

It has often been said that we love most in life what we have lost. The Poles have lost their cherished land with its mountains and forests and plains and lakes many times in their turbulent history. It is that history that has shaped their character, defined their present, and given them hope and determination as they face a promising, but still uncertain, future.

NOTES

1. Norman Davies, *God's Playground: A History of Poland*, Vol. II (New York: Columbia University Press, 1982), p. 16.
2. James Michener, *Poland* (New York: Fawcett Crest, 1984), p. 53.
3. "Poland Invites," The Polish Tourist Information Center.
4. *The New York Times*, October 3, 1993.

2

The Rise and Fall of Poland (Prehistory to 1918)

*A*ccording to legend, an ancient tribe led by three brothers once wandered across what is now the continent of Europe. One day they entered a land of unsurpassing beauty. One brother, Lech, saw an eagle in its nest and took it as a good omen. "This is where we should settle," he said to his brothers, Czech and Rus.

They disagreed with him and the tribe split into three groups, each led by one brother. Czech took his tribe westward and settled what later became Czechoslovakia. Rus went east and settled what is today Russia. Lech and his tribe stayed in what was to became Poland. He founded a city on the spot where he saw the eagle and called it Gniezno, "nest" in Polish. Gniezno later became the first capital of Poland and is today a thriving city. The white eagle became the symbol of Lech's tribe and remains the symbol of Poland to this day.

This fanciful tale may be legend, but it contains more than a germ of truth. The earliest people to inhabit eastern Europe were Slavic tribes, and they originally settled in the thick forests of Poland and western Russia about 2,000 B.C. From this base they spread out, gradually settling in what is today the Czech Republic, Slovakia, the Balkans, Greece, and Germany.

One of the largest Slavic tribes in Poland were the Polanie, which literally means the "people who live in the field." They called the land they lived in Poland. In their primitive communities called *grody*, the Polonie and their neighbors grew grains, raised domestic animals, and established a simple form of government run by tribal chieftains. Gradually, their little communities grew into towns and cities. One of these *grody* eventually became the city of Poznan in west-central Poland, the nation's oldest continually inhabited city.

Poland's First Dynasty— The Piasts

The Polanie came to dominate the other tribes and organized them into separate individual states. The first great Polonie ruler was the legendary Piast, of whom little is known other than that he founded Poland's first dynasty of kings. Piast's great-great grandson, Mieszko I, is the first historic prince of Poland. He ruled from A.D. 963 to 992 and is known for two great accomplishments—uniting the tribes of Poland into a nation and accepting Christianity for his country.

Mieszko's religious conversion was partially political. Although a separate country, Poland was under the domination of the German Teutonic tribes to the west. By accepting Christianity, Mieszko could count on protection against the Germans from the Holy Roman Empire, an empire in western-central Europe founded by Charlemagne, king of the Franks, in 800.

Growth of Poland

Poland in 1386, at time of union with Lithuania

Lithuania in 1386, at time of union with Poland

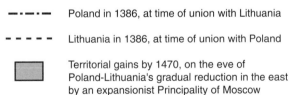

Territorial gains by 1470, on the eve of
Poland-Lithuania's gradual reduction in the east
by an expansionist Principality of Moscow

The Roman Catholic Church also brought Western culture to Poland, putting it on a different path of development from Russia and other neighboring countries, which developed traditions more Eastern than Western.

Mieszko's son Boleslaw the Brave, who succeeded him in 992, was an even more adept ruler than his father. He strengthened the ties among the tribes under him, made peace with the Germans who were still a threat, and extended Poland's territory. In 1025, Boleslaw felt powerful enough to declare himself king. Unfortunately, he died the same year. As often happens in hereditary monarchies, Boleslaw's sons did not have his gift for state building. They quarreled among themselves for power and carved Poland up into small kingdoms. Unable to defend themselves, these kingdoms courted disaster. Over the defenseless plains rode a series of invaders—Germans, Russians, Czechs, and most dreaded of all, the Mongolian Tatars.

These invaders often left total devestation in their path. Here, novelist James Michener describes a Tatar attack on a Polish village in 1241 in his historical novel *Poland.*

> Like an explosion of lava from a volcano, the horsemen swept over the settlement, setting fire to every cottage, slaying every human being they encountered, even killing cattle too old to be herded easily to that night's campsite, wherever it was going to be. Of those Bukowo peasants trapped inside the village, all were slain, even though not one of them had taken arms against the Tatars or tried in any way to oppose them.[1]

By the early 1300s, however, two strong leaders emerged to reunify a people who now shared a common language and religion. Wladyslaw the Short (reigned 1305–33) and his son Casimir the Great (1333–70) reformed the Polish kingdom and helped shape its culture by encouraging the arts. Casimir, who established a single system of money and founded the University of Kraków, is today considered one of Poland's greatest kings. An old saying claims "He found a Poland made of wood and left behind one made of stone."[2]

Casimir died without an heir—the last of the Piast kings. His kingdom fell into the hands of his nephew, King Louis of Hungary. Louis had little interest in Poland or its people, and ruled with benign neglect. He had no sons and the Polish nobles, fearing they would face political chaos on his death, made an unusual decision. They demanded that Louis's 9-year-old daughter Jadwiga (see boxed biography) succeed him as Poland's ruler. Two years later, Louis died and Jadwiga was crowned "king" in Krakow, one of the few female monarchs in modern European history.

What followed is a star-crossed romance out of a fairy tale. Jadwiga was in love with an Austrian prince named Wilhelm, but Poland's nobles decided on a more politically useful mate for her. Neighboring Lithuania, on the Baltic coast, was at war with Poland, and the Polish nobles wanted to make peace between the two countries and join them against a common enemy—the Teutonic Knights of Germany. To this end, they forced Jadwiga to give up Wilhelm and become engaged to Lithuanian Grand Duke Ladislas Jagiello. Jadwiga was 12 and the Grand Duke 32 at the time. For the good of her country, Jadwiga agreed to the marriage. On his part, Jagiello agreed to accept Christianity.

Poland's "Golden Age"

Jagiello proved to be a good husband and an even better ruler. Although Jadwiga died in 1399, Jagiello ruled Poland for another 35 years. In 1410, he led the Poles and Lithuanians in one of the great military victories of medieval Europe, defeating the Teutonic Knights in the Battle of Gruenwald.

He described the memorable battle in a letter to his second wife, Anna of Cilli:

> On Tuesday, the Feast of the Apostles, the Grand Master [of the Teutonic Knights] with all his power drew close to your forces, and demanded that battle be joined. . . . After we had stood and watched each other for a time, the Grand Master sent two swords over to us with this message: "Know you, King . . . , that this very hour we shall do battle with you. For this, we send you these swords for your assistance." We replied: "We accept the swords you send us, and in the name of Christ, before whom all stiff-necked pride must bow, we shall do battle." At which, with the troops standing in full order, we

Queen Jadwiga

(1370–1399)

She is considered by many to be the Polish Joan of Arc, although she never led an army into battle and did not die a martyr to a cause. She might, in fact, have ended up merely the pawn in an international game of power politics, but thanks to her strength of character and deep love for her country she became much more than that.

Jadwiga was a princess by birth, daughter of Louis the Great of Hungary and Elizabeth of Bosnia. Her father had inherited the Polish throne and treated his distant subjects with indifference. The Poles wanted a ruler to follow Louis that would be their own and pressured the Hungarian monarch, who had no sons, to enlist one of his daughters as their next "king." Jadwiga got the job by default—one elder sister died and the other was being groomed for the Hungarian throne.

Leaving her homeland for a new and strange country was only Jadwiga's first sacrifice for Poland. A political marriage to Grand Duke Jagiello of Lithuania was the second. The joining of Poland and Lithuania strengthened both countries and helped create a Polish empire that would flourish for nearly two centuries.

Although her marriage to Jagiello reduced Jadwiga's power as monarch, she continued to co-rule with him and was his wisest counselor. Her two greatest achievements as queen were negotiating a peaceful settlement with the warlike Teutonic Knights to the west and the rebuilding of the University of Kraków which had been founded by her great-uncle, Casimir the Great.

The birth of her son in 1399 was a joyful event, producing the first male heir to the Polish throne in decades. Tragically, the child died, and Jadwiga, weak and despondent, died soon after at the age of 29. She did not live to see her beloved university reopen nor the great flowering of Polish culture under her husband's dynasty. Yet, she is still remembered today as a woman of great faith, gentleness and peace.

advanced to the fray without delay. Among the numberless dead, we ourselves had few losses. . . . We cut down the Grand Master, . . . forcing many others to flee. . . . The pursuit continued for two miles. Many were drowned in the lakes and rivers, and many killed, so that very few escaped. . . .[3]

Jagiello's victory secured his power and created a new dynasty of Jagiellonian kings who ruled Poland for about 200 years. This period from 1410 to 1572 is known as Poland's "Golden Age," and for good reason. Under the Jagiellonians, Poland grew from a nation-state to an empire. Poland controlled the rich Ukraine, a province of Russia, and other Russian lands. Polish art and literature reached new heights.

The Jagiellonians established a national parliament called the Sejm in 1493, the year after Columbus reached America, making Poland one of the first European countries to establish democratic traditions. Twelve years later it adopted a constitution, granting limited rights to all Polish citizens. This "democracy" was a far cry from the democracy enjoyed in the United States and other countries today. The Sejm was selected by the king and nobility from their own numbers. But this first important step toward representative government was far more advanced than any taken by the monarchies which then existed in France, Germany, and Russia.

This new freedom, however, had its down side. If even one member of the Sejm disagreed with a proposed law, all he had to do was stand up and say "*nei pozevlom*" (I disapprove), and the law could not pass. This prevented most laws from ever passing and often reduced the parliament to a quarreling, ineffective body. Nevertheless, the nobles jealously guarded what power they had and a fatal pattern of weak, ineffective kings emerged that would bode ill for their nation in the years ahead.

When Sigismund Augustus II, another childless monarch, died in 1572, the nobles of the Sejm decided that rather than let one of their own number become king, they would elect a foreign king. A foreigner, they reasoned, would be lax in his long-distance rule and allow them more room to exert their own authority. So in 1587, Sigismund III Vasa, king of Sweden, became king of Poland. It was a grave mistake that signaled the end of the golden age and started Poland on a downward spiral that would continue for centuries.

Nicolaus Copernicus (Mikolaj Kopernik) ̄

(1473–1543)

The man known as "The Father of Astronomy" was born in the city of Thorn, now called Torun, in north central Poland. His father died when he was ten and he was raised by an uncle, who was a city cathedral official

R. Cooper sculp.ᵗ

"The Father of Astronomy," Copernicus divided his life between science and the church, where he served as a high clergyman. His theory that placed the Sun, not Earth, at the center of the solar system was controversial, and he only agreed to publish his findings near the end of his life.
(The New York Public Library Picture Collection)

and later a bishop of the Catholic Church. The church appeared to be the career path for Copernicus as well, although he became seriously interested in astronomy during his student days at Jagiellonian University in Kraków.

Most astronomers still accepted the 1,300-year-old theory of the Greek scientist Ptolemy, which said Earth was the unmovable center of the universe and that all the heavenly bodies moved around it. Copernicus, however, believed this was untrue. He spent the remainder of his life proving, by observation of the moon and planets, that Earth, like the other planets, rotated around the Sun.

After his studies, Copernicus was appointed by his uncle as the canon, or head clergyman, of Warmia Cathedral in Frombork, Poland. A man of indefatigable energy, he managed to perform his church duties while working on his astronomical experiments and earning a degree as a medical doctor. In his spare time, Copernicus developed Poland's first standard currency to fight growing inflation. His plan was, unfortunately, rejected by the government.

Copernicus knew full well that the church and state would be even less tolerant of an attack on Ptolemy's theory, which kept humankind at the center of the universe. He wisely kept his own theory a secret, while writing down his ideas in a book called *De Revolutionibus Orbium Coelestium*, Latin for *Concerning the Revolutions of the Celestial Spheres*. When news of his book and its revolutionary theory leaked out, Copernicus, now an old man of 70, finally agreed to have it published. He only saw the finished book on his deathbed. Copernicus's book blazed the way for such modern astronomers as Galileo Galilei and Johannes Kepler to probe the stars and planets.

"The theory of the Earth's motion is admittedly difficult to comprehend," Copernicus wrote in his great work. "But if God wills, I shall . . . make it clearer than the Sun . . ."[4] He did, shedding light on the universe and ushering in the modern scientific age.

The Long Decline

Poor leadership, internal squabbling, and wars with its neighbors weakened the Polish government until it was unable to govern its empire. The Ukrainians rebelled in 1648 and won their independence from Poland. In 1655, Sweden grasped control of Poland's Baltic provinces. But then a common enemy united the rivaling states. The Islamic Turks advanced into Poland, intent on taking it over along with the rest of central Europe.

King John Sobieski (reigned 1674–96), one of Poland's strongest rulers in the 17th century, led a brazen assault against the Turks in Austria at the historic Battle of Vienna in 1683. He dealt them a resounding defeat that saved not only Poland but all of Europe from Turkish rule. It was one of Europe's most decisive battles; however, it did not save Poland from its other enemies. When Sobieski died in 1696, the Sejm elected the next king from German Saxony. This incensed the descendants of Sobieski, who won the support of Poland's neighbors in the War of the Polish Succession (1733-35). This war, in which Polish soldiers played only a marginal role, ended in victory for the Saxon king, Augustus III.

The Three Partitions

By greedily keeping power unto themselves, the Sejm once again brought their country to the brink of disaster. By 1772, Russia, Austria, and Prussia, the largest of the German states, made a treaty to seize a chunk of Poland for each of them. Russia took part of eastern Poland, which became Byelorussia. Austria grabbed much of southern Poland. Prussia took the section known as Pomerania in western Poland. Together, the three took a third of Poland's territory and half of its people in what has come to be called the First Partition.

The Poles rose angrily against their enemies. In 1791, the government produced a new constitution that ended the Sejm's "liberum vote," granted more personal freedoms, and gave the vote to many more Poles. It was a much-needed reform, but it came too late. Poland no longer had the military might or strong leadership to save itself from its more powerful

This woodcut commemorates King John Sobieski's victory over the Turks at the Battle of Vienna in 1683. The Turks' defeat ended their plan to conquer Europe, but Poland's fortunes fell soon after at the hands of other enemies. (The New York Public Library)

Tadeusz Kosciuszko

(1746–1817)

"He is as pure a son of liberty as I have ever known,"[5] said Thomas Jefferson of this Polish nobleman who fought for freedom on two continents.

Tadeusz Kosciuszko was born into an old but poor noble family and studied at the Royal Military School in Warsaw. His ambition was to be a soldier, and he went to France to study military engineering. When he returned to Poland in 1774, he worked as a tutor for the daughter of a Cossack leader. The romantic young man fell in love with his student and barely escaped her father's wrath with his life.

He fled to France and then America, a land in as much turmoil as Poland. The cause of American freedom from Britain moved Kosciuszko deeply, and he offered his services as a volunteer to the Philadelphia Congress. They immediately made him a colonel of engineers. Kosciuszko's contribution to the American Revolution was critical. He helped win the battle of Saratoga with a brilliant defense plan, designed and built the fortress at West Point, which still stands, and served as chief engineer of the Continental Army's southern forces. For his loyal service, he was rewarded at the war's end with land, an annual pension, the rank of brigadier general, and United States citizenship.

Kosciuszko returned to Poland in 1784, hoping to see his land win the same freedom his adopted country had. He fought in the war of 1791, which ended in Poland's defeat and the loss of much of its territory.

Three years later, Kosciuszko led against the Russians the valiant insurrection that bears his name. Leading peasants wielding scythes, he beat the Russians at Raclawice on April 4, 1794. But the Russians outnumbered the Poles and defeat once again was inevitable. The Third Partition saw

neighbors. In fact, the reforms actually hastened the country's downfall. The monarchies of Russia and Prussia feared Poland's democratic reforms might spread to their own countries. In 1793, the Second Partition of Poland saw these two countries carve up more of the nation to the west and the east.

Poland disappear from the map of Europe. Kosciuszko was wounded and captured at the bloody battle of Maciejowice in October. He was imprisoned in St. Petersburg's Peter and Paul Fortress for three years. Czar Paul pardoned the Pole in 1797 and he traveled to London, a man without a country.

Kosciuszko returned to America, where he collected his accumulating pension and used it to finance plans for Polish independence. He returned to Europe to raise support for the struggle, but received little encouragement. A broken, lonely man, Kosciuszko settled in Switzerland, where he died at age 71. In his will he asked that his lands in America be sold and the money used to buy black Americans out of slavery. It was the final legacy of a man who believed passionately in the cause of freedom for all people.

A dashing figure, as seen here in his military garb, Kosciuszko was called the "Hero of Two worlds" because of his involvement in the American Revolution and the one he later led in his native Poland.
(The New York Public Library Picture Collection)

The Poles rose up in arms the following year to take back their territory. They were led by the courageous General Tadeusz Kosciuszko (see boxed biography), who had fought in the American Revolution 15 years earlier. Like many uprisings in Poland before and since, the rebellion of 1794 was a valiant effort, but a doomed one. Outnumbered and outweaponed, the Poles lost and Kosciuszko was captured and imprisoned by the Russians.

The following year the process that began over two decades earlier drew to its bitter conclusion. Russia, Prussia, and Austria divided the remains of the Polish state among themselves. The population of the Polish lands, which included Lithuania, shrunk from 14 million at the time of the First Partition to a mere 6 million at the time of the Third Partition. Poland ceased to exist as a political entity. It disappeared from the map of Europe. Its neighbors had obliterated a country that had existed for a thousand years.

A Nation of Exiles

But the Polish people would not be obliterated so easily. They kept the flame of Polish freedom burning in their minds and hearts, both at home and abroad, where many went during these difficult years. Throughout the 19th century, they kept the idea of Poland alive through their art, music, and literature, most notably in the passionate patriotic piano compositions of Frédéric Chopin (see boxed biography, Chapter 3) and the stirring poetry of Adam Mickiewicz (1798–1855). Perhaps no Pole better expressed the defiant spirit of his conquered nation than Mickiewicz when he wrote these words:

> Poland said: "Whosoever will come to me shall be free and equal, for I am FREEDOM." But the Kings when they heard were frightened in their hearts, and said . . . "Come, let us slay this nation." And they conspired together . . . And they crucified the Polish Nation, and laid it in its grave, and cried out "We have slain and buried Freedom." But they cried out foolishly . . .
>   For the Polish Nation did not die. Its body lieth in the grave, but its spirit has descended into the abyss, that is into the private lives of people who suffer slavery in their country . . . But on the third day the soul shall return again to the body, and the Nation shall arise, and free all the peoples of Europe from slavery.[6]

For a brief moment, the Poles' romantic idealism found a champion in the century's first great figure, French ruler and conqueror Napoleon Bonaparte. With expatriate soldiers in his ranks, Napoleon recaptured

Polish lands taken by Prussia and "returned" them to the Poles under the name the Grand Duchy of Warsaw. But, in fact, Napoleon controlled the Grand Duchy in all but name. In the end, it was just another one of his conquests. After his fall from power in 1815, the land returned to Prussia. As a kind of cruel joke, the Russians decided to name one part of their Polish lands the "Kingdom of Poland," but it remained in firm Russian control.

Among Poland's masters, only Austria allowed the Poles to keep their language and culture. Russia and Prussia mercilessly suppressed the Polish way of life among its people. Polish schools were strictly run by their masters. The daughter of Manya Sklodowska, who would later become world famous as the Nobel Prize–winning chemist, Madame Curie, describes a visit from a Russian inspector to her mother's school in Warsaw in 1878.

> M. Hornberg, accepting the chair offered him by Mlle Tupalska, seated himself heavily.
>
> "Please call on one of these young people."
>
> In the third row Manya Sklodovska instinctively turned her frightened little face toward the window. . . .
>
> But she knew very well that the choice would fall upon her. She knew that she was almost always chosen for the government inspector's questioning. . . .
>
> At the sound of her name, she straightened up. . . .
>
> "Your prayer," snapped M. Hornberg . . .
>
> Manya recited "Our Father" in a voice without color or expression. One of the subtlest humiliations the Tsar [Russia's king] had discovered was to make the Polish children say their Catholic prayers every day *in Russian.* . . .
>
> "Who rules over us?"
>
> To conceal the fire of their eyes, the directress and the superintendent stared hard at the registers they held before them. As the answer did not come quickly enough, Hornberg, annoyed, asked again in louder tones:
>
> "Who rules over us?"
>
> "His Majesty Alexander II, Tsar of All the Russias," Manya articulated painfully. Her face had gone white.[7]

The Poles were not always able to "conceal the fire" they felt inside. There were uprisings in 1830, 1840, and 1863—all of which failed.

World War I and Independence

As the 19th century drew to a close, however, a new and charismatic Polish leader named Jósef Pilsudski emerged. Pilsudski, a Socialist, spent five years in exile in Siberia for agitating. In 1892, he returned to Russian Poland and founded a left-wing, patriotic newspaper, *Robotnik* (The Worker). When World War I broke out in 1914, Pilsudski led a legion of 10,000 Polish troops who fought on the Austrian side against the Russians. Pilsudski became a national hero but was interned by the Germans, the Austrians' allies, in 1917 because they didn't trust him. This led the Poles to the grim realization that despite the different sides Austria, Germany, and Russia fought on, they were still united in their oppression of Poland.

In 1918, Germany and Austria lost the war. The empire they had built up over two centuries fell to pieces. Roman Dmowski, another Polish leader, founded a Polish National Committee in Paris. He lobbied fervently for the Allied powers of the United States, France and England to help form an independent Poland.

The Americans were deeply sympathetic to the Polish cause. Many Poles had emigrated to America in the late 1800s and early 1900s, and had contributed greatly to their new homeland. United States President Woodrow Wilson made Polish independence one of the conditions of the armistice treaty. Jósef Pilsudski was chosen to head up the new and independent Poland. After nearly 125 years of subjugation, a new Poland emerged from the ashes of the Great War. The future held great promise, but it also held great challenges.

NOTES

1. James Michener, *Poland* (New York: Fawcett Crest, 1984) p. 40.
2. Christine Pfeiffer, *Poland—Land of Freedom Fighters* (Minneapolis, Minn.: Dillon Press, 1984), p. 45.
3. Norman Davies, *God's Playground: A History of Poland*, Vol. I (New York: Columbia University Press, 1982), p. 123.
4. Arnold Madison, *Polish Greats* (New York: David McKay Co., 1980), p. 8.
5. Carol Greene, *Poland* (Chicago: Children's Press, 1983), p. 101.
6. Davies, op. cit., pp. 8–9.
7. Eve Curie, *Madame Curie*, trans. Vincent Sheean (New York: Da Capo Press, Inc., 1986), pp. 19-21.

3

Poland Under Democracy, Nazism, and Communism (1918 to 1980)

*P*oland was a free country again after over a century of foreign domination, but independence brought a new host of problems. Putting Poland back together was a little like putting back together Humpty Dumpty. The Allies helped Poland reclaim territory from Germany and Austria, but Russia, now controlled by the Communists after the Russian Revolution of 1917, refused to turn over its Polish lands. The conflict quickly led to war.

"By attacking Poland," reasoned Russian leader Vladimir Lenin, "we are attacking also the Allies. By destroying the Polish army we are destroying the Versailles settlement."[1] It was, however, the Soviets who were defeated in the short war, and under the Treaty of Riga, signed in 1921, Russia returned at least some of its Polish territory.

The new Polish republic declared its lofty ideals in the invocation to its new constitution, that was passed on March 17, 1921:

> We, the people of Poland, thanking Providence for freeing us from one and a half centuries of servitude, remembering with gratitude the bravery, endurance, and selfless struggles of past generations, which unceasingly devoted all their best energies to the cause of Independence . . . striving for the welfare of the whole, united, and independent mother-country, and for her sovereign existence, might, security, and social order, and desiring to ensure the development of all moral and material powers for the good of the whole of regenerated mankind and to ensure the equality of all citizens, respect for labour, all due rights, and particularly the security of State protection, we hereby proclaim and vote this Constitutional Statute in the Legislative Assembly of the Republic of Poland.[2]

Achieving these goals, however, would not be easy. A century of separation had made Poles in the three partitioned sections strangers to one another. The ideal of a free Poland was something they had yearned and fought for decades. Now that it had become a reality, that chronic reluctance to give up individual independence for the good of all once again asserted itself. According to a 1931 census, a little less than 70 percent of the population was Polish. The remaining inhabitants were Ukrainian, Jewish, Byelorussian, and German. They clamored for recognition and more rights.

It was a daunting challenge, even for a strong leader like Jósef Pilsudski, to get these diverse groups to agree on anything. In its first eight years, the new Poland had no fewer than 13 different governments, each appointed by an increasingly disillusioned Pilsudski. The economy was also in shambles—antiquated, ineffective, and unjust. Three quarters of the population worked in agriculture and were mostly peasant farmers. Industrial workers in cities made up only 17 percent of the population. The remaining tiny percentage—professionals, entrepreneurs, and land-owners—held all the wealth and power.

From Democracy to Dictatorship

In 1923, Pilsudski resigned in disgust as premier. Three years later, he led a military coup and marched into Warsaw, taking the city. The watchword of his coup was *sanacja*—a moral "cleansing" of the state that would end corruption, limit the power of the Sejm, and strengthen the power of the executive branch of government. On May 31, 1926, Pilsudski was elected president of Poland. In effect, he became his country's dictator.

If Pilsudski was a dictator, however, he was a relatively benign one. He used his power to stabilize the economy, secure the state, and improve relations with other nations. His goodwill campaign culminated in a loan of $172 million in 1929 from the West, most of it from the United States.

Pilsudski remained in power until his death at 68 in May 1935. One of his last acts was to adopt a new constitution that limited the powers of the president. His successors found it more difficult to keep control of the country, which soon was beset by protests and strikes. Polish Communists and right-wing conservatives struggled for power, leaving little room for the moderate leaders to maneuver. Meanwhile, events outside Poland were taking an even more ominous turn.

After a decade of economic ruin and political flux following its defeat in World War I, Germany had chosen a new leader who promised a brighter future—Adolf Hitler. Hitler rebuilt German economic and military strength through the mid-1930s. In 1938, he demanded that Poland return the port city of Gdansk, which had previously been the German city of Danzig. Poland refused. Hitler now had the excuse he had been looking for to go to war.

World War II

At dawn on September 1, 1939, Hitler's troops invaded Poland. Great Britain and France, who had pledged to defend Poland, declared war on Germany two days later. World War II had begun.

Once again, the Poles fought tenaciously against the invaders, but they proved no match for the all-powerful Nazi war machine. German planes

Ignace Jan Paderewski

(1860–1941)

Hearing the young Polish pianist play, the celebrated Viennese piano teacher Theodor Leschetizky said, "It is too late. Your fingers lack discipline. You can never become a great pianist."[3] But the young Pole believed otherwise. Ignace Jan Paderewski worked hard and in three years embarked on a career as a concert pianist that would make him one of the world's most renowned virtuosos.

In 1891, Paderewski made his first memorable concert tour of the United States. He would return 19 times. Outside of playing the piano, his passions were billiards, bridge, and the cause of Polish independence.

Paderewski gave away so much of his wealth to worthy causes, including the Polish nationalistic movement, that he had to come out of semiretirement and return to public playing to make money, in spite of a serious nervous disorder. During World War I, he toured North and South America, raising money for his war-racked country.

"I came to speak to you of a nation which is not yours," he would declare to spellbound audiences, "in a language which is not mine."[4] It was Paderewski who personally persuaded U.S. President Woodrow Wilson to include independence for Poland in his Fourteen Points for a peace treaty.

When the war finally ended, the distinguished Pole was chosen to be his country's premier and minister of foreign affairs. Within a year, he resigned from both posts, unable to cope with the political intrigue of the new Poland.

and bombers obliterated the Polish Air Force in 48 hours. When German tanks rumbled across the countryside, they were met by a division of Polish cavalry armed with lances and sabers. Warsaw, the capital, surrendered on September 27, after 60,000 of its residents had been killed.

Ten days earlier, Soviet leader Joseph Stalin, who had signed a secret pact with Germany not to interfere with the Polish invasion, invaded Poland from the east. After a mere 21 years of independence, Poland was once again a conquered land.

The Germans divided their share of Poland into four districts, overseen by a Nazi governor-general who made his headquarters in Kraków. About

Paderewski returned to his first love, the concert stage, until he suffered a heart attack during an American tour in 1939. When Hitler invaded Poland later that year, Paderewski was appointed president of the Polish parliament in exile. He died two years later, while back in America raising money and support for his homeland.

The great patriot, composer, and musician was buried in Arlington National Cemetery in Washington, D.C. He requested that his heart be returned to Poland when his country became free once more.

Besides being a great pianist and composer, Paderewski helped form the new Polish nation after World War I and served as its first premier. (The New York Public Library Picture Collection)

a million Poles and Polish Jews were deported from their homes and over 700,000 Germans sent to settle in their annexed lands.

The Russians made eastern Poland a part of Soviet Byelorussia and the Ukraine. In August 1940, Stalin declared Lithuania, once a part of the Polish empire, a republic of the Soviet Union, which it remained for the next half century.

Hitler's grand plan for Poland was a simple and brutal one. He would kill all the Jews, who he blamed for Germany's problems, and reduce all other Poles to the status of slaves. To enact this plan, he turned Poland into a killing ground. Concentration camps, vast prisons meant for the extermination of their inmates, were built in the once grassy countryside. Three of the most notorious Nazi death camps—Auschwitz, Treblinka, and Majdanek—were established in Poland, primarily so Poland's three and a half million Jews would not have to be transported very far to be exterminated.

At first, many non-Jewish Poles also went to the Nazi gas chambers, along with Gypsies and other Europeans. This practice later stopped, and these Poles were put to work in the camps. A remarkable firsthand account of the gas chambers at Auschwitz is provided by Sophia Litwinska, a Polish prisoner:

> About half-past five in the evening [Christmas Day, 1941] trucks arrived and we were loaded into them, quite naked like animals, and were driven to the crematorium. . . . The whole truck was tipped over in the way they do it sometimes with potatoes or coal loads, and we were led into a room which gave me the impression of a shower-bath. There were towels hanging round, and sprays, and even mirrors. I cannot say how many were in the room altogether, because I was so terrified, nor do I know if the doors were closed. People were in tears; people were shouting at each other; people were hitting each other. . . . and suddenly I saw fumes coming in through a very small window at the top. I had to cough very violently, tears were streaming from my eyes, and I had a sort of feeling in my throat as if I would be asphyxiated. I could not even look at the others because each of us concentrated on what happened to herself.[5]

Incredibly, Litwinska was snatched from the gas chamber by Nazi guards and saved, because, she believed, she had come from a Lublin prison and had been sent there by mistake.

Among those Poles not sent to the camps were two and a half million who were transported to Germany to work in labor camps. Another 200,000 Polish children were found to be "racially valuable" by the Nazis and sent to Germany to be what they called "Germanized"—trained to be good Germans.

Those Poles left in the occupied nation continued to resist. When the Germans took over Warsaw, they forced all remaining Jews into one section of the city and walled it off from the rest of Warsaw. In April 1943, the Nazis attempted to remove the 60,000 Jews left in the Warsaw Ghetto to concentration camps. The Jews resisted. Armed with only knives and

The devastation visited on Poland during World War II is grimly captured in this photograph of Warsaw taken in 1946. The only object left intact in the shattered landscape is a traffic sign. Over 90 percent of the city was destroyed.
(The Bettmann Archive)

stones, they fought their Nazi masters with a fierce and desperate will for a month. In the end, 56,000 of them died. Those few thousands who survived were executed. A handful miraculously managed to escape and told the world of one of the war's most heroic episodes.

While underground activity and sabotage inside Poland went on, those Poles fortunate enough to have fled before and during the invasion joined the Allied efforts in France and Great Britain. A Polish army in exile was formed with 85,000 soldiers. When France fell to the Nazis, they fled to England. Poles continued to fight valiantly in the North African campaign and the Battle of Britain.

Marie Curie (Manya Sklodowska)

(1867–1934)

She is perhaps the most distinguished Polish woman in modern times, but like so many of her 19th-century countrymen and women, she spent her entire career outside of her war-torn homeland. Marie Curie received two Nobel Prizes for her scientific work, the first person to do so.

She was born Manya Sklodowska in a middle-class Warsaw family. Her father was a science professor, her mother, a musician. Manya could read at the age of four and graduated first in her class at 15. To pay her way through university, she worked as a governess during the day and attended classes at night.

She studied math and science at the world-famous Sorbonne in Paris for a year. There she met the well-known scientist Pierre Curie, who had devised a law of magnetism, which was named for him. Curie fell in love with the intensely ambitious young woman and they married in 1895. They became partners in work as well as in love and made a close study of radiation given off by the newly discovered radioactive substance uranium.

The Curies were confounded by the fact that uranium ore contained more radioactivity than the refined uranium. Where did the rest of it go? they asked themselves. They painstakingly extracted tiny amounts of radioactive elements from tons of uranium ore. The first new element they named polonium, in honor of Marie's homeland. The second element was discovered quite by accident.

When Marie returned to their ramshackle laboratory one evening in 1902, she saw a row of test tubes giving off an eerie bluish glow. They called the substance radium. For their discovery of these elements, the Curies shared the Nobel Prize in physics in 1903 with Antoine Henri Becquerel, discoverer of natural radioactivity.

Pierre Curie died in a tragic street accident in 1906, and his wife took his place on the faculty at the Sorbonne, becoming the first woman to hold the position of teaching master. In 1911, she won her second Nobel Prize, in chemistry, for her work isolating radium. Three years later, she helped found the Radium Institute, where she served as director.

During World War I, Marie Curie showed the beneficial use of radiation, helping to x-ray wounded soldiers at the front with her daughter Irene. This tireless scientist was still hard at work when she died in 1934. Her death was diagnosed as due to pernicious anemia caused by years of exposure to the substance she had spent much of her life studying—radium.

Poland's greatest scientist, Marie Curie (Manya Sklodowska) won the Nobel Prize twice—once in physics and once in chemistry. She is seen here (left) in old age with her daughter. (The New York Public Library Picture Collection)

In June 1941, the Germans began a full assault on the Soviet Union, taking Stalin by surprise. The Russians now became part of the Allied cause, with the Nazis their common enemy. The Russians were completely driven from Poland, which was now all in German hands.

But Hitler had taken on too many enemies. His army suffered its first major defeat in Russia and was forced to retreat. By mid-1944, the tide of war had turned dramatically. The Germans were losing and the Poles took heart. In August, the entire city of Warsaw rose up in rebellion. Their aim was twofold—to drive out the Nazis and keep the Russians from coming in. By now, the Russians had begun to advance westward, liberating Polish territory from the Germans. They called themselves the Polish Committee of National Liberation (PCNL), the only legitimate power in Poland.

The Germans managed to hold the Russians back at the Vistula River and laid siege to Warsaw. An already devastated city was reduced to rubble. The Germans bombed Warsaw from the air and on the ground. In two months, they killed 200,000 people and leveled 90 percent of the buildings. The Soviets, who could have come to the aid of the Poles, had orders from their leader, Joseph Stalin, to wait outside the city and watch.

The extent of the suffering of the people of Warsaw can be glimpsed in this appeal written by Polish women to Pope Pius XII:

> Most Holy Father. . . . For three weeks, while defending our fortress, we have lacked food and medicines. Warsaw is in ruins. The Germans are killing the wounded in hospitals. They are making women and children march in front of them in order to protect their tanks. There is no exaggeration in reports of children who are fighting and destroying tanks with bottles of petrol [gasoline]. We mothers see our sons dying for freedom and the Fatherland. Holy Father, no-one is helping us. The Russian armies which have been for three weeks at the gates of Warsaw have not advanced a step. The aid coming to us from Great Britain is insufficient. The world is ignorant of our fight. God alone is with us. Holy Father, Vicar of Christ, if you can hear us, bless us Polish women who are fighting for the Church and for freedom.[6]

Only when the Germans had done their worst, did the Soviets move in and "liberate" what was left of Warsaw.

The wages of war were higher in Poland than in any other nation, except for the Soviet Union. Six million Poles had died, half of them Jews.

Of that total, only 600,000—500,000 of them civilians—died in military confrontations. The nation's population had dropped by nearly a third of what it was at the war's start. Hundreds of towns were to be repopulated by Poles previously exiled to Russia and elsewhere. Polish intellectuals and Jews had been nearly exterminated. Other minorities had been uprooted by the war. What was left was a vast majority of Roman Catholic Poles.

The Communist Era

Disillusioned by the failure of their government to prevent the slaughter, some Poles turned to communism as the best blueprint for Poland's future. This political doctrine called for a classless society where workers shared in the products of their labor. The development of national communism in Poland fit in well with the plans of Stalin, who, like Hitler, dreamed of dominating Europe.

With the defeat of Germany and the end of the war, the Soviets were deeply entrenched in Poland, Czechoslovakia, Hungary, and much of the rest of Eastern Europe. The Soviet-controlled PCNL was running the Polish government, with Wladyslaw Gomulka, leader of the Communist Polish Workers' Party, as premier.

The Allies, pressured by the Polish national government in exile, agreed to recognize the Polish government if it included non-Communist political groups. The Soviets agreed, but only for a while. By 1948, the Communist Party of Poland, supported by the Soviets, was in complete control of the country. To make their domination complete, the Soviets installed Konstantin Rokossovsky, a Russian military officer, as Polish minister of defense.

Those Polish Communist leaders who resisted Soviet influence were removed from power. Even Gomulka himself was forced to resign his post in 1948 and later put under house arrest. The following year, a new constitution was adopted, a carbon copy of the Soviet constitution. Personal freedoms disappeared. Books and films were heavily censored. Agriculture and industry were taken out of the hands of individuals and controlled by the state.

But, just as they had resisted the Germans and countless invaders before them, the Poles defied the Communists. The Catholic Church, led by Stefan Cardinal Wyszynski (see boxed biography in chapter 6), was in the forefront of the resistance movement. In 1952, the cardinal began a three-year prison term, but the Poles continued to protest. In 1956, riots broke out in the ancient city of Poznan. Fifty thousand people marched in a demonstration and a Communist security police officer was lynched. Soviet tanks were sent in to restore order and over fifty people were killed and 200 wounded.

A poem by Polish writer Adam Wazyk, published the previous year, expresses the anger and frustration of the Polish people under the yoke of communism. Here is an excerpt:

> there are exhausted people dying from heart attacks;
> there are people slandered and spat upon,
> people assaulted on the streets
> by common hoodlums, for whom legal definitions can't be found;
> there are people waiting for a scrap of paper;
> there are people waiting for justice;
> there are people who wait a long time.[7]

Nikita Khrushchev, Stalin's more moderate successor in the Soviet Union, looked for a practical solution to the Polish problem. He wisely allowed Gomulka to return to power, realizing he was the only leader who could bring the people together. Khrushchev paid a visit to Warsaw in October 1956 and received Gomulka's assurance that he would not break off relations with the Soviet Union.

In what came to be called the "Polish October," Gomulka instituted reforms in the rigid Communist system to make it more acceptable to the people. Farmers were given back their land and Polish Catholics were allowed to worship openly. Rokossovsky was removed from power and sent back to Russia. Cardinal Wyszynski was released from prison. Gomulka and Wyszynski worked out a pact of mutual cooperation. Life in Communist Poland became somewhat better, but Poles continued to protest and demonstrate for more freedom into the 1960s.

By 1970, the situation had again worsened. When steep food price increases were announced on December 12, thousands of workers at the Lenin shipyard in Gdansk, a hotbed of worker unrest, marched to party

This 140-foot (43m) steel monument is a dramatic memorial to the 55 workers killed by police during the "bread riots" in Gdansk in 1970. It was unveiled at the city's Lenin shipyard on the tenth anniversary of the tragedy. Solidarity was organized the same year.
(The Bettmann Archive)

headquarters to protest. Two days later, a general strike began. When demonstrators refused to disperse, police opened fire. Here is what happened as described by one shipyard striker who was there:

One of the commanders, the lieutenant, just simply shot at the crowd with his pistol. It was about an arm's length from me, and I only realized what had happened when I saw this squirt of blood. One of the lads from the shipyard had been hit straight in the larynx, in the artery, and the blood—you know—it spouted up about four feet. It was oil on the flames, as we say in Polish: the people saw it, and they threw themselves at the police cordon. Then there was a massacre . . .[8]

The unrest quickly spread to other cities in the country. Gomulka was unable to control the situation and was replaced as Communist Party head by a likable ex-miner, Edward Gierek. Gierek tried to talk to the workers in their own language and reminded them that he had been a worker, too, and knew how they felt. Gaining a certain amount of cooperation from the workers, he made some positive reforms. He further improved relations with the church and forged stronger ties with non-Communist countries. But the economy, mismanaged by the Russians for two decades, continued to decline. Ordinary Poles could afford little more than the basics of life, and food prices soared higher and higher. Only when riots erupted in 1976 did the government put a halt to price increases.

Foreign loans, initiated by Gierek, had ended some of the country's pain, but, by 1980, Poland was unable to pay back the loans and was deep in debt. Unrest grew throughout the land. Again, it found its focal point in Gdansk, where shipyard workers and others banded together to form a trade union. Their leader was a 37-year-old unemployed electrician named Lech Walesa. They called their union movement Solidarity.

NOTES

1. *Encyclopaedia Britannica,* 1965 ed., Vol. 18, p. 133.
2. Norman Davies, *God's Playground: A History of Poland,* Vol. II (New York: Columbia University Press, 1982), p. 402.
3. R. Kent Rasmussen, *The People's Almanac,* No. 3, p. 461.
4. Carol Greene, *Poland* (Chicago: Children's Press, 1983), p. 107.
5. John Carey, ed., *Eyewitness to History,* pp. 554–555.
6. Davies, op. cit., pp. 478–479.
7. Quoted in ibid., p. 582.
8. Neal Ascherson, *The Struggles for Poland* (New York: Random House, 1987), p. 181.

The Downfall of Communism and a Free Poland (1980 to 1993)

Solidarity gave the Polish people an organization from which to build a national base of resistance to the Communists and a platform to get out their message. That message started as specific to the workers of 50 trade unions in Gdansk, but under the skillful leadership of Lech Walesa, an electrician turned union organizer, it soon spread to encompass all the grievances of the Polish people—political, economic, social, and spiritual.

The Rise of Solidarity

During the long, hot summer of 1980, thousands of workers went on strike to protest the government's announcement that some meat prices would rise nearly 100 percent. "We must tell the people the truth regarding the disastrous situation of the country," wrote Mieczyslaw Rakowski, editor of *Polityka.* "A program of radical reform is urgently needed."[1] From Warsaw to Lublin to Gdansk the strikes spread.

The government had dealt with strikes before, but this was something else. Walesa had organized millions of workers and supporters. The

Solidarity began as an organization of labor unions and quickly grew to involve millions of Poles who wanted freedom from communism. This June 1983 demonstration in Krakow followed a service held by Pope John Paul II during a visit to his native city. (The Bettmann Archive)

possibility of a general strike that could paralyze the entire nation was chillingly real.

On August 31, the government and the strikers came to an agreement in a Gdansk conference hall. The government recognized the Gdansk workers as a free and independent union with the right to strike. It promised workers better working conditions and health standards, less censorship, and Saturdays off. It even allowed workers to listen to radio broadcasts of Catholic Mass as they worked.

The idea of an organization of workers' unions was not unusual in the West, but in an Eastern Bloc country in 1980, it was nothing less than revolutionary. No group of workers under Soviet communism had ever been able to form an independent union separate from the state.

Edward Gierek, who had weathered many a political crisis in his 10 years in power, was seen as an ineffective leader by his Soviet masters and unable to deal with the unrest that led to the formation of Solidarity. In September 1980, he was forced to resign and was replaced by Stanislaw Kania, a leading minister who had previously headed the army and the secret police.

A few weeks later, the delegates of 36 independent unions from throughout Poland met in Gdansk and united, calling themselves "Solidarity." When the organization attempted to legally register itself with a Warsaw court, the court delayed the action. It later asked the union to recognize the Communist Party and its "leading role" in Poland. Solidarity refused and gave the government until November 12 to recognize it or face a general strike. Two days before the deadline, the government backed down and granted Solidarity its charter without the language change. It was the first time a labor organization, independent of the Communist Party, had been recognized in a Communist country.

If the government thought it could contain Solidarity by legitimatizing it, it was mistaken. On December 14, 1980, a thousand farmers gathered in Warsaw to form their own power base. They founded Rural Solidarity, demanding the same rights and privileges as the industrial workers of Solidarity. When the government held up the registration of the new organization, the farmers staged a sit-in in the city of Rzeszów that lasted into February. When Solidarity came to the support of the farmers, the government agreed to negotiate. Although recognition did not come, Rural Solidarity held its first congress in Poznan in west-central Poland in March

Lech Walesa

(1943–)

One of modern Poland's great success stories, this son of a carpenter rose to become a leader in his people's struggle for freedom. Lech Walesa went from being a jailed dissident to president of his nation in a few short years. In as short a time, he went from being a national hero to a distrusted politician, whose popularity in a recent poll was lower than the man he helped overthrow, General Jaruzelski. Whatever can be said about Lech Walesa, he stirs strong emotions in Poles, both for and against him.

He was born in Popaw during the Nazi occupation, one of eight children. On the death of his father, his mother married her brother-in-law and died in a traffic accident while visiting relatives in the United States. Lech's stepfather decided to stay in America rather than return to Communist Poland.

Walesa went to state vocational school and later got a job as an electrician in Gdansk's Lenin shipyard. When 55 shipyard workers died in the "bread riots" of December 1970, Walesa's life was changed. He became a leading labor organizer, working to negotiate with the government for better working conditions and pay for the shipyard workers. In 1976, he was fired over a protest and spent years drifting from job to job trying to make a living for his family while continuing his work as a labor leader.

In January 1979, Walesa cofounded a free trade union on the Baltic coast and helped publish the first issue of a radical journal, *The Worker of the Coast*. In August, a strike among shipyard workers won Walesa reinstatement as a worker. As the strike continued, Walesa's demands included political rights as well as economic ones. On August 31, 1979 he signed the Gdansk Agreement, giving workers in an Eastern Bloc country, for the first time, the right to form unions and strike.

Placed under house arrest for 11 months during Poland's period of martial law, Walesa emerged from this dark time apparently repentant,

1981. The same month, the police broke up a sit-in of Rural Solidarity members in Bydgoszcz, about fifty miles northeast of Poznan, and three people were seriously injured. Solidarity threatened a nationwide strike unless the guilty parties were punished. Soon after, Rural Solidarity was officially recognized by the government.

although not for long. In October 1982, he won the Nobel Prize for Peace and became a figure of international fame. During the time of change in the Soviet Union in the mid-1980s, Walesa's power and influence continued to grow, until he helped negotiate free elections with the Communists in 1989. In December 1990, his country now independent and the Communists out of power, Walesa became the first freely elected president in Poland in over 50 years.

Although his tenure as president has alienated many of his supporters, Walesa has proven himself to be a leader who cannot be counted out, whatever the odds against him. "I don't know anyone who would dare say he would win next year," said one sociology professor. "But he may create certain political situations that allow him to win. One of his opponents used to say he's a genius at solving problems he created himself."[2]

A national hero during the 1980s as the leader of Solidarity and champion of Polish rights, Lech Walesa's popularity has plummeted since he became president of an independent Poland.
(The Bettmann Archive)

To illustrate how far the government had sunk, in a June poll, the top three most respected institutions in Poland were the Catholic Church, Solidarity, and the army. The Communist Party ranked 14th. When the first anniversary of the Gdansk accords arrived, Solidarity's membership numbered 10 million.

In September, Solidarity's First National Congress of Delegates convened in Gdansk with the celebration of mass by Archbishop Jozef Glemp, the newly named primate of Poland. Glemp succeeded Cardinal Wyszynski who died in May. When the first session of the congress ended with a letter of support to workers in the Soviet Union and Eastern Europe, the Soviets branded the congress "an anti-Socialist and anti-Soviet orgy."[3] The danger of Solidarity's fever of freedom spreading was now seen as an imminent threat to the Communists.

The Polish government faced a serious dilemma. If it gave in any more to the unions, it could jeopardize the future of the state and provide a model for the peoples of other Eastern Bloc countries to imitate. In October, Kania was replaced by the prime minister, General Wojciech Jaruzelski, a man the Soviets felt was moderate enough to deal effectively with Solidarity without giving away any more power.

Martial Law

In an unheard of move, Walesa, Jaruzelski, and Archbishop Glemp had a summit meeting to talk about how they might work together to bring Poland out of its crisis. However, further talks made little headway as the economy grew grimmer and grimmer. Economic figures released in November showed industrial production down 15 percent from the previous year. Solidarity's leadership supported the call from its Warsaw chapter for a nationwide day of protest on December 17, but the protest never took place.

During the night of December 12, Polish troops, under orders from General Jaruzelski, sealed off Poland's cities. All telephone and telegraph lines within the country were cut. The leaders of Solidarity, in Gdansk for a national meeting, were rounded up by police and arrested.

On a sunny Sunday morning, Poles woke up to their darkest day since the Communist takeover in 1948. Martial law had been declared by General Jaruzelski. All public gatherings were banned, all civil rights suspended, a 10:00 P.M. to 6:00 A.M. curfew was declared, all schools were closed, and over 10,000 people, including Lech Walesa, were detained or imprisoned.

The suddenness of the government's action caught the people off guard. The sight of tanks in the streets reminded many Poles of the grim days of World War II. Strikes and demonstrations continued, but now they were met with bloody reprisals from the police and army. The Polish ambassador to the United States, Romuald Spasowski, stated that "a cruel night had spread over my country" and defected to the United States.

Gradually Poland's borders were reopened and communications reestablished, but "temporary" martial law continued for nearly a year. In October 1982, Jaruzelski officially outlawed Solidarity. Only a few brave members of parliament opposed the motion, including future Prime Minister Hanna Suchocka.

Jaruzelski released some of the union leaders, and by 1984 they were all released. He hoped they had learned their lesson and would not attempt to threaten the state's authority again. But the government's actions had only increased the determination of the leaders of Solidarity to continue the struggle for political and economic freedom.

The movement received two boosts in its efforts from abroad. In October 1982, the very month that Solidarity was outlawed, Lech Walesa won the Nobel Peace Prize. In acknowledging Walesa's peaceful efforts to bring about democratic change in his country, the world put further pressure on the Polish government to reform itself. Then in June 1983, John Paul II visited his homeland for the third time since becoming pope. A fervent advocate for Polish freedom since his days as a priest, the pope met with both Jaruzelski and Walesa and worked as a mediator between the two. With Solidarity outlawed, the church in Poland had taken over the role of the nation's conscience and called repeatedly for the full reinstatement of civil rights.

Jaruzelski may have banned Solidarity, but he could not ban the yearning for freedom it had stirred in the hearts of the Polish people. Demonstrations soon began again, with the firm support of the Catholic Church.

In October 1984, a heinous crime brought the Polish people to their feet in protest. Father Jerzy Popieluszko, a young radical priest in north Warsaw and a strong supporter of Solidarity, was abducted and murdered by a gang of secret police. Jaruzelski denied that his government was responsible for the murder and put the killers on public trial. The murderers claimed they had been encouraged by senior officials, although no one else was charged in the case. Half a million Poles poured into Warsaw to attend the funeral of the martyred priest. "Rest in peace," Lech Walesa said at the funeral. "Solidarity is alive, because you have given your life for it."[4]

Then change in the Soviet Union made change in Poland all but inevitable. In 1985, Mikhail Gorbachev came to power in Moscow and began a series of reforms to open up Soviet society, end corruption, and promote economic growth. To improve the economy, Gorbachev made sharp cuts in military spending and loosened the stranglehold the Soviets had on their Eastern Bloc neighbors. As the Soviet Union focused on improving life at home, it pulled back its influence in these other Communist countries. This only further served to undercut the authority of the Communist government in Poland and gave Jaruzelski, who argued his actions were only meant to prevent a Soviet invasion of Poland, room to negotiate with Solidarity.

The First Free Elections

In early 1989, thanks to the efforts of Solidarity and the earth-shattering changes in the Soviet Union, the unthinkable happened. President Jaruzelski agreed to sit down at the bargaining table with Solidarity. A series of roundtable talks began. Walesa pressed the government to agree to the holding of free and open elections in which Solidarity candidates could run against those put forth by the Communist Party. In April 1989, the two sides signed accords that once again made Solidarity legal and paved the way for the first free elections in Poland since World War II. The people would vote for delegates to serve in a two-house parliament and a president to be elected for a six-year term. The agreement would give the Communists 38 percent of all parliamentary seats in the lower house and 35 percent to members of Solidarity. The remaining 27 percent of the delegates would come from numerous smaller political parties. There would be no quotas for the upper house or senate. All 100 seats were up for grabs and Solidarity hoped to get a majority of them.

Walesa emerged from the negotiations as a major power to be reckoned with. ". . . for the first time we have talked to each other using the force of arguments, and not arguments of force," he said. "It bids well for the future, I believe, that the roundtable discussions can become the beginning of the road for democracy and a free Poland."[5]

Surprisingly, Walesa himself did not run as a candidate in the elections scheduled for June 1989. He preferred to coordinate activities behind the scenes, although he expressed interest in running for president in 1995.

As the elections drew closer, the Communists found themselves, for the first time in their lives, having to compete for votes with other political parties. Many Communists claimed they were not opposed to reform. Even Jaruzelski himself now seemed to welcome it. Like Gorbachev, however, he hoped to keep it within the scheme of a Communist system of government.

"The majority [of Communists] are in the middle, and they are waiting to see whether the reforms will succeed," said Liberal Party member Ludwick Kusecki. "If they succeed they will be with us . . ."[6]

June 4, election day in Poland, was anticipated with hope around the world. Poland was the first of the Eastern Bloc countries to move toward democracy, and it was not expected to be the last. The government of Hungary was also inching toward reform. And while the Communists held tenaciously onto East Germany, Czechoslovakia, Romania, and Bulgaria, the people of these countries looked hopefully to Poland.

When the voting was over, Solidarity had won a resounding victory. While the Communists, as predicted, held a majority in the lower house, Solidarity delegates swept into the Senate, taking 99 of the 100 seats. The Communists were further embarrassed by the results of some elections where candidates ran unopposed but still failed to get the 50 percent of the vote needed to win. Jaruzelski squeaked into office as the new president by one vote in parliament. Many Solidarity members abstained, refusing to vote for a former Communist adversary.

July 4, 1989, America's Fourth of July, was a historic day in Poland as well, for on that day, Solidarity delegates marched proudly into the parliament building. They had come from being outlaws in their country to being its legitimate lawmakers. How they would use their new-found power was a matter of intense debate. Some wanted to make the Communists pay for the 40 years of misery they had inflicted on Poland. More moderate members wanted to work with the Communists and gain their support in facing the daunting challenges of political and economic reform that lay ahead.

Jaruzelski was ready to negotiate. On July 25, he met for two hours with Walesa, but the Solidarity leader rejected his offer of a coalition. Why, Walesa reasoned, should he join up with the Communists when Solidarity was now "those forces that enjoyed the support of a majority of society."[7]

Jaruzelski, who had pledged in his role as president of a new Poland to resign as Communist Party head, was replaced by the country's prime minister, Mieczyslaw Rakowski. The new prime minister who replaced Rakowski was a man who many Poles despised. Czeslaw Kiszczak had been interior minister in the early 1980s and supervised the establishment of martial law and the arrest of many Solidarity leaders. Within two weeks, Kiszczak resigned under pressure, and Solidarity organizer Tadeusz Mazowiecki, a Catholic lawyer and journalist, became the first non-Communist head of an Eastern Bloc government since the end of World War II. "I think we can gather our strength from within ourselves," Mazowiecki said soon after taking power. "This is not easy, but it is possible if everyone begins to realize and to feel that we are now on our own, and that it all has some sense and can lead somewhere."[8]

In November, Lech Walesa went to the United States, where he addressed a joint meeting of Congress. Walesa made an impassioned plea for foreign aid, aid that would be desperately needed if Poland were to change from a Communist economy to a free market one.

We have heard many beautiful words of encouragement. These are appreciated, but being a worker and a man of concrete work, I must tell you that the supply of words on the world market is plentiful but the demand is falling. Let deeds follow words now . . . It is now worth recalling this great American plan which helped Western Europe to protect its freedom and peaceful order [the Marshall Plan]. And now it is the moment when Eastern Europe awaits an investment of this kind—an investment in freedom, democracy, and peace, an investment adequate to the greatness of the American nation.[9]

The Downfall of Communism and the Division of Solidarity

As Poles increased their own investment in their new, bright future, it became increasingly apparent that the Communist Party would not be part of that future. Under more and more pressure from the people and their representatives in the new parliament, the Communist Party of Poland voted to disband itself on January 28, 1990. At about the same time, the government, led by Prime Minister Mazowiecki, declared a program of

As communism weakened, national protests become more intense. This violent confrontation between police and protesters occurred outside the Palace of Culture in Warsaw during the last Congress of the Polish Communist Party in January 1990. (The Bettmann Archive)

radical economic reform that would move Poland from the poorly planned economy of the Communists to a free-market economy such as in the Western democracies. On January 1, 1990, price controls were lifted and prices of food and other products skyrocketed. Bread rose an average of 40 percent in one week. Electricity rose 400 percent and coal 600 percent. A tank of gas cost more than many Poles earned in a week.

At the same time, state enterprises were "privatized," sold off to private individuals or groups, and subsidies, financial assistance, to government businesses were abruptly ended. These businesses were pushed into bankruptcy and workers were paid unemployment compensation until they could find new jobs. Jeffrey Sachs, the Harvard professor hired as a consultant by the new government, called this new approach to changing the economy "shock therapy."

By September, another major shock wave swept the halls of government. Jaruzelski, the man who saw the June election as "a huge step toward democracy," was pushed out by that same democratic movement. He resigned from his office and new presidential elections were set for the end of the year.

But if communism had crumbled, the movement that had brought about its end was splintering. Solidarity no longer reflected the meaning of that word. With the goal of independence achieved and communism dead, there was no common enemy to fight. As Walesa himself pointed out before the election, "What was needed were politicians, not dissidents, and politics has to do largely with compromise."[10] But compromise was not easy to find among the dozens of political parties that sprang up in the wake of communism. The diversity of opinion was admirable, but it stymied any kind of consensus for the future of the new nation.

Prime Minister Mazowiecki found his chief rival in the December 1990 election for president was none other than Lech Walesa himself. The two men now stood on opposing sides—Mazowiecki, the first intellectual to support Solidarity, representing the politicians and technocrats, and Walesa, the man of the common people, standing for labor and the more conservative Catholic section of the organization. Walesa won the election and was sworn into office on December 22, 1990. It was the first completely free election in Poland in more than half a century, and Walesa was the first popularly elected president in that time.

Poland's struggle for freedom was finally over. But the new challenges of changing over to a democracy, politically and economically, were just beginning. Walesa's choice for prime minister, Krystof Bielecki, kept the economic reforms moving full steam ahead. The privatization of state businesses forged forward and over a million new jobs were created in the private sector. But the downfall of the Communist economy put millions of other Poles out of work. For the first time in decades, Poland faced a serious unemployment problem. Shock therapy was shocking the people out of their complacency and hope was being replaced by fear of an unknown future in the brave new world of a free-market economy.

The Democratic Union versus the Democratic Left Alliance

When the first fully free parliamentary elections were held in October 1991, voter turnout was only 42 percent. The parliament they elected was a fractured and fragmented body representing 29 political parties. Walesa appointed a coalition government, but it fell apart without support in the parliament by June 1992. The president tried to put another prime minister, Waldemar Pawlak, into office but failed to get enough support for him. Instead, Hanna Suchocka, head of the Democratic Union Party (see boxed biography) was chosen as a compromise candidate who was popular with all sectors of the parliament. She became the first female prime minister in Eastern Europe in the 20th century.

A longtime dissident against the Communists, Suchocka proved her commitment to economic reform by keeping the shock therapy in place. She also showed she had the backbone needed to run the country by standing up to striking workers in May 1992. But economic reforms continued to raise unemployment and create misery. Suchocka's coalition alliance with the church, which under communism would have been admired, was now bringing sharp criticism. The church's paternal role in Polish life, especially in politics, was less acceptable in a free Poland than it had been under communism. The government backed the church ban against abortion with legislation and earned the resentment of millions of Poles.

As the Democratic Union came under attack, the former Communists regrouped. They now called themselves the Democratic Left Alliance and

Hanna Suchocka

(1946–)

It's a bit like mushrooms after the rain," said Poland's first female prime minister. "Solve one problem, and the next day, two, four, eight spring up."[11]

Head of the Democratic Union Party, Hanna Suchocka dealt effectively with a host of problems until, after a little less than a year in office, the radical economic reforms she promoted were rejected by the Polish people and she was forced out of office.

Suchocka was born in Pleszew, a village in western Poland where her father was a pharmacist and leading citizen. She studied constitutional law at the University of Adam Mickiewicz in Poznan. Upon graduating in 1968, she was hired as a junior faculty member and offered the opportunity to join the Communist Party. She flatly refused. "I decided that I wanted to be an independent person,"[12] she said. Instead, she joined the small Democratic Party, which the Communists allowed to exist.

As Polish dissatisfaction and resistance to the Communists grew, Suchocka grew with it. She joined Solidarity soon after its founding in August 1980 and was elected to parliament as a Democratic Union member. When Solidarity was silenced during martial law, Suchocka was one of the few brave legislators who voted against the outlawing of the organization. Realizing she was in a tiny minority, she retired from parliament and public life in 1984.

When communism collapsed in Poland in 1989, Suchocka was reelected to parliament and became one of the leading politicians of the new post-Communist Poland. After a succession of prime ministers, she was offered the job in the summer of 1992. As the only politician in the land who had the support of both conservatives and moderates, Suchocka

put themselves forward as a viable alternative to the shock therapy of the reformers. They promised change, too, but at a slower pace that would not cause undue hardship to the common people.

Surprising as it seemed, the once reviled Communists now appeared to be a comforting link with the past for many Poles. "The former became an effective leader who could stand up to striking workers just as she had stood up to Communist bureaucrats.

While her government's radical economic reforms put Poland in the forefront of Eastern European countries, they created strong resentment among many Poles who were tired of sacrificing for a future good. In May 1993, her government fell by a single vote in parliament. In the next parliamentary elections in September, the Democratic Left Alliance, made up of former Communists, came into power, vowing to modify reforms.

Hanna Suchocka remains an important opposition leader and an active spokesperson for economic change. "Poland is the first in the region in which the reforms are having effect," she said shortly before the 1993 election. "We can't lose this."[13]

The first modern woman prime minister in Eastern Europe, Hanna Suchocka's government grew unpopular due to its alliance with the Catholic Church and its steady pursuit of a free-market economy. Here she is welcomed to a united Germany by Chancellor Helmut Kohl.
(The Bettmann Archive)

Communists are the only ones who can really make order out of this mess," said Jan Binkowski, a former baker. "They have experience. In the forty years when we had Communism, we did rebuild, we did achieve something. In the past four years, we've driven unemployment up to four million, closed a lot of state enterprises and ruined a lot."[14]

One of the people held most responsible for Poland's problems was the former champion of Solidarity, Lech Walesa. His failure to form a workable government was blamed largely on his own thirst for power and desire for control.

"He's like a commemorative statue," declared worker Henryk Grosiask. "When it's first welded and shining, people come to see it but after a while it stops shining and people stop coming."[15]

Another observer, sociologist Wojciek Pawlak, summed up Walesa's fatal flaw more perceptively: "His strength is turning people against something or someone. He can't very well turn the people against himself now that he is the highest public official."[16]

But in September 1993, when the election results were in, that appeared to be exactly what Walesa and his new "non-party movement for reform" did. The Left Alliance took 20 percent of the vote, the Polish Peasant Party, a Socialist-leaning group, gained 16 percent, the Democratic Union came in third with about 10 percent, and Walesa's Nonparty Bloc took a meager 5 percent. The people had spoken.

Alliance leader Aleksander Kwasniewski, was expected to become the new prime minister, but the job went instead to a 34-year-old farmer's son, Waldemar Pawlak, who had served briefly as prime minister once before. Pawlak's Polish Peasant Party formed a coalition with the Alliance. "I want the material well-being to be revealed not in statistics," Pawlak told the nation, "but in every Polish home."[17] This was the kind of language the people understood.

Poland had led the way toward freedom in Eastern Europe in 1989. Now, four years later, it was leading the way back toward the familiar. Former Communists were also beginning a comeback in Hungary, Bulgaria, and Romania.

Perhaps the most startling aspect of the Communist comeback was not that so many Poles wanted it, but that few of them had any fear of what it might lead to. As President Walesa said after the election, "Nothing can happen because we have democracy, a free press, magnificent youth . . ."[18]

A new day had dawned in Poland. Not even the Communists were to be feared. There were still problems to be faced and obstacles to be overcome, but freedom ruled in a land that had so often only known it as an ideal.

NOTES

1. Lawrence Weschler, *Solidarity: Poland in the Season of Its Passion* (New York: Simon & Schuster, 1982), p. 169.
2. *The New York Times*, July 6, 1994.
3. Weschler, op. cit., p. 191.
4. Neal Ascherson, *The Struggles for Poland* (New York: Random House, 1987), p. 227.
5. Bernard Gwertzman and Michael T. Kaufman, eds., *The Collapse of Communism* (New York: Times Books, 1990), p. 35.
6. Ibid., p. 113.
7. Ibid., p. 126
8. Ibid., p. 130.
9. Ibid., pp. 207–208.
10. Ibid., p. 36.
11. Stephen Engleberg, "Her Year of Living Dangerously," *The New York Times Magazine*, September 12, 1993, p. 38.
12. Ibid., p. 55.
13. Ibid., p. 41.
14. *The New York Times*, September 12, 1993.
15. *The New York Times*, September 19, 1993.
16. Ibid.
17. *The New York Times*, October 28, 1993.
18. *The New York Times*, September 25, 1993.

5

Government

---

*U*nder communism, the Polish government was run by 7 percent of the people, those Poles who belonged to the Polish United Workers Party, also known as the Communist Party. The one-house legislature consisted of 460 members, the vast majority of them Communist members. When the Sejm was not in session, 17 of its members, forming the Council of State, ran the government. A prime minister, 8 deputy prime ministers, and 20 ministers who ran government departments, composed the Council of Ministers, appointed by the Sejm. In effect, the "Polish People's Republic" was a republic in name only. It was run by a small hierarchy within the Communist Party.

The Three Branches of Government

Today, some of these same Communists are back in power, but the structure of the government they run is radically different from what it was under communism. The first free elections, held in June 1989, created a new legislative body made up of two houses—an upper house, the Senate, consisting of 100 members and a lower house, made up of the 460 members as in the previous government. In the first election, the Communists were guaranteed a certain number of seats in the lower house, but that changed in the next election, held in July 1990.

A revised constitution in June 1990 called for a new executive branch—a president to be elected by the people. The president's role, however, unlike in the United States, was seen as subordinate to that of the prime minister, who actually runs the government with his ministers.

The first session of the new Polish Senate, which convened in 1989, made for some strange bedfellows. Solidarity leader Lech Walesa (center) and Communist leader Wojciech Jaruzelski (left) share a joke during the Senate's first session. A little over a year later, Jaruzelski would step down as president, to be later replaced by Walesa in a free election. (The Bettmann Archive)

The president can appoint a prime minister, although his choice is subject to the approval of the parliament. The president is also involved in foreign policy and has veto power over legislation proposed by parliament. His veto can be overturned by a two-third majority of parliament.

On the local level, government is run by councils that are elected every four years. The country is divided into 49 provinces called voivodships, or in Polish, *wojewodztwo*. These voivodships are divided into 822 towns and 2,121 wards, or *gmina*. The councils run local services with money from a combination of local and central government taxes. District agencies help link local councils with the central government.

The third branch of government, the judiciary, is headed by a Supreme Court in Warsaw that hears final appeals on cases and oversees the legal system. Under that is an administrative Supreme Court and a Court of Appeals. Under Communism, there were no jury trials in Poland; all decisions were made by judges, appointed for five-year terms. District courts handle most civil and criminal cases. County courts handle more serious or important cases. There are also 65 family consultative centers, set up in 1977, to handle domestic relations and divorce. Ordinary courts began to handle divorce cases, which are on the rise in Poland, in 1990. District court judges are elected, while Supreme Court judges are appointed by the president from candidates proposed by the National Council of the Judiciary.

An Unpopular President

There have been five different governments in Poland in the aftermath of communism. No other Eastern European country has had so many in that five-year period. The one political constant in most of that time has been President Lech Walesa. But Walesa's popularity has dropped steadily in recent years. "The former union leader . . . has transformed himself into an emblem of broken promises, a character driven by power rather than a savior of the underclass,"[1] wrote the *New York Times*.

President Walesa has proven an embarrassment to many Poles who cringe at his bad grammar and his constant maneuvering to play king-maker in government. Others are angered by his expensive tastes at a time when many Poles are suffering severe economic hardships. He

Poland

recently moved into a renovated 17th century palace, although the presidential residence was fine.

Although Walesa has declared himself a candidate for a second five-term in 1995, in a June 1994 poll only 5 percent of the people surveyed said they would vote for him.

A Suspect Government,
A New Prime Minister

Walesa's political future may hinge on the fate of the present government, run by the coalition of the Democratic Left Alliance and the Polish Peasant Party. Under Prime Minister Waldemar Pawlak, the government has promised to better meet the needs of the people, while keeping economic reforms moving forward. So far, it has had a mixed record. While movement toward a free-market economy shows no signs of halting, other moves in the political arena are making people question the government's commitment to change.

In August 1994, Marion W. Zacharski, a former Communist, was nominated to head Polish intelligence. Zacharski had been a spy for Poland during the Cold War, and, in 1981, was arrested in the United States and sentenced to life imprisonment. He was freed four years later in an exchange with Western agents being held by the Soviets. President Walesa challenged Zacharski's appointment, claiming it would endanger Poland's relationship with the United States and seriously hurt any chance of the nation becoming a member of NATO. Zacharski quickly resigned, but the damage was done. "If we were rebuilding the Warsaw Pact*, this appointment would be justified," said Bogdon Boruszewicz, an opposition member of parliament.[2]

The same week, two Polish generals who had allegedly given the orders for the murder of Solidarity priest Jerzy Popieluszko back in 1984, were acquitted by a panel of five judges. The announcement of the verdict was met with cries in the courtroom of "Communist cover-up!" One of the

*The Warsaw Pact was an organization of six Eastern European countries, all Soviet satellites at the time, and the Soviet Union, formed in 1954. The members agreed to assist each other in the event of an armed attack on one of their members.

judges, however, admitted the generals "were probably responsible for the murder,"[3] but they could not be convicted for a lack of evidence.

The most serious threat to Poland's democratic reforms came in September, when the lower house passed the Official State Secrets Act. Under this act, journalists or anyone else disclosing information vital to Poland's interest in 71 categories could be sentenced to up to 10 years in prison. The new law, which later passed in the upper house, was not only condemned by liberals, but even by the Democratic Left Alliance's own house organ, which claimed the act would create "a gray zone that permits the Government to cover up incompetence or abuse of power."[4] Some wondered if the act was a reaction to the crusading journalist who, since 1990, had uncovered rampant corruption among government officials involved in embezzlement and smuggling.

In February 1995, the growing conflict between President Walesa and Prime Minister Pawlak, whom Walesa accused of delaying economic reforms, came to a head. Under threats from Walesa that he would dissolve parliament unless a new prime minister was found, Pawlak resigned. He was replaced by Jozef Oleksy, previously the Speaker of parliament and a senior member of the Democratic Left Alliance. Oleksy, 48, was minister in charge of trade unions under the last Polish Communist government. While a far more experienced politician than Pawlak, Oleksy is not expected to set a new agenda for the ex-Communist government.

"I don't foresee any dramatic changes with the new prime minister. In a sense it's just trading places,"[5] said politics professor Edmund Wnuk-Lipinski of the Polish Academy of Sciences.

If the new government is to regain the confidence and support of the people, it will have to assure them of their good intentions by continuing the difficult transition from authoritarianism to true democracy.

NOTES

1. *The New York Times,* July 6, 1994.
2. *The New York Times,* August 19, 1994.
3. *The New York Times,* August 20, 1994.
4. *The New York Times,* September 17, 1994.
5. *The New York Times,* February 8, 1995.

6

Religion

*T*o say that Poland is a Catholic country is about as much of an understatement as saying the pope is Catholic. (The pope is also Polish.) Roughly 95 percent of the population is Roman Catholic. The Polish people, particularly in the villages and rural areas, are among the most devoutly religious Catholics in the world.

In 1978, Polish Catholicism took on a new meaning for the world. Karol Cardinal Wojtyla, Archbishop of Kraków, was elected Pope of the Roman Catholic Church. As John Paul II, he became the first non-Italian pope in over 450 years and the first Polish pope ever. Even more importantly, John Paul was the first pope from a Communist country. The effect that had in Eastern Europe, and particularly in Poland, was extraordinary.

A year after becoming pope, John Paul visited his homeland and called on the Communist government to allow more freedom to the people. This speech inspired millions of Poles to resist the Communists and gave particular hope and courage to one man—Lech Walesa, leader of the labor group Solidarity.

Stefan Cardinal Wyszynski

(1901–1981)

If the Catholic Church is the soul of the Polish people, the soul of the church for three decades was Cardinal Wyszynski. This beloved head of the Polish church defended his faith from the Communists, learned to accommodate them to survive, and lived to see the rebirth of new hope for his people with the coming of Solidarity.

Wyszynski was born in the village of Zuzela in Russian-occupied Poland. He was ordained a priest on his 23rd birthday and became vicar of the basilica at Wloclawck. Wyszynski's commitment to social causes as well as religious ones became quickly evident. He earned a doctorate in

The leader of the Polish Catholic Church during some of its darkest days, Cardinal Wyszynski resisted the Nazis and did what he could to accommodate the Communists without sacrificing the church's authority.
(The Bettmann Archive)

sociology and canon law at the Catholic University at Lublin. For a time, he edited a Catholic daily newspaper and wrote several books about labor issues.

When World War II broke out, the fearless priest worked against the Nazis in the Warsaw underground. In 1946, a year after the war's end, he was made bishop of Lublin. Three years later, Wyszynski rose to the highest office of the church, primate of Poland, at the very moment the Communists were taking over his country.

Although Wyszynski made an uneasy alliance with the Communists, he knew they would do everything to break his power and that of the church. When he was elected a cardinal in November 1952, he refused to go to the Vatican to be consecrated, fearing he might not be allowed back into Poland. The following year, he was arrested at home by the secret police. When his faithful dog bit the hand of one of the arresting officers, the cardinal carefully bandaged the wound before being taken away. He spent three years in prison without ever coming to trial.

In 1956, one of the first acts of the new prime minister, Wladyslaw Gomulka, was to release Wyszynski from prison. The pragmatic Communist and the equally practical cardinal formed a long-lasting pact of cooperation. Gomulka gave the church more freedom than it enjoyed in any other Soviet Bloc country, and the cardinal supported the "national communism" of Gomulka's government.

For all his compromising, Wyszynski remained the staunch defender of the faith and resisted the new Communist leadership when Gomulka was replaced in 1970. A decade later, the aged cardinal gave support and encouragement to the reform-minded workers' union, Solidarity. His influence helped to bring about the eventual collapse of communism in his country, an event he did not live to see.

Catholicism was first introduced in Poland in A.D. 966. Since then, the church has become an integral part of Polish society and culture and has been called the very soul of the Polish people. It was the church that gave Poles the support and faith to withstand endless hoards of invaders from the Mongols to the Soviet Communists. When Poland ceased to exist as a country at the end of the 18th century, the church sustained the people and gave them hope when all hope seemed lost. ". . . the history of the Roman Catholic Church provides one of the very few threads of continuity

Few nations are as Catholic as Poland, where 95 percent of the population belongs to this religion. Here, young girls and their parents line up outside a church in Torun for their first Holy Communion ceremony. (Connie Grosch/ Impact Visuals)

in Poland's past," writes historian Norman Davies. "Kingdoms, dynasties, republics, parties, and regimes have come and gone; but the Church seems to go on forever."[1]

Unlike previous conquerors of Poland, the Communists were atheists who opposed religion. In their first eight years in power, they did everything they could to suppress the church. They threw priests and higher clerics into prison. They shut down churches, banned religious education, and restricted religious practices. But nothing could destroy the faith of the Polish people. The church had stood by them in times of crisis. Now they would stand by the church.

By 1956, the Communists realized they were fighting a losing battle. They ended the persecution and allowed religious worship to resume largely unhampered. The church was given more latitude than in any other Communist country in Eastern Europe.

The Black Madonna of Czestochowa

To gain a better appreciation of the depth of the religious faith of Polish Catholics, one should visit Czestochowa, Poland's holiest city, in south-western Poland. It is the home of the Black Madonna, a holy painting, supposedly done by Saint Luke and brought to a monastery on Jasna Gora, Mountain of Light, in the 14th century. The centuries have darkened the faces of the Virgin Mary and her child, the baby Jesus—hence, the name Black Madonna. According to legend, the monastery was attacked by Swedish soldiers during their invasion of Poland in 1655. Soldiers defended the monastery for 40 days until the invaders mysteriously retreated the day after Christmas. The Polish people attributed the miraculous retreat to the Black Madonna and rose up to beat back the Swedes from their land. Each year, tens of thousands of Catholic Poles make the pilgrimage to the monastery during the yearly feast held in honor of Our Lady of Czestochowa.

Polish Jews

Despite its long Catholic heritage, Poland has for centuries welcomed people of all faiths, making it one of the most tolerant countries in Europe. Their own difficult history has made the Poles sensitive to all of society's victims and outcasts, especially those who have fled persecution for religious beliefs. Most prominent among these believers are the Jews.

Jews once made up 10 percent of the population of Poland, numbering 3.5 million. They included well-to-do peasants, artisans, and merchants, who could be found in every Polish city and town. The vast majority of Poland's Jews were killed in the Holocaust. Many others emigrated to escape extermination in the death camps. Today, there are only 5,000 Jews left in Poland.

Despite their spirit of tolerance, Poles have also been guilty of anti-Semitism in the past, as have the people of nearly every European nation. Some Poles have even been accused of being indifferent to the plight of their Jewish neighbors during World War II. But there were many

Poles who risked their own lives to help, too. Tadeusz Pankiewicz, a pharmacist in Krakow, is one outstanding example.

Pankiewicz was ordered by the Nazis in 1941 to leave Kraków's Jewish ghetto where his store was located. Somehow, he persuaded the Germans to let him stay, so he could continue selling medicine to the sick. Risking his life, he hid Jews in his pharmacy and stored sacred Torah and other Jewish artifacts in a vault under his store. When the war ended, Pankiewicz was a witness for the prosecution at the Nuremberg trials where leading Nazis were prosecuted for war crimes.

Another hero of the Holocaust was Father Maximilian Kolbe, a Polish priest who took the place of a condemned man, a gentile, at Auschwitz. Kolbe has recently been canonized as a saint by Pope John Paul.

Before the Holocaust of World War II, Jews made up 10 percent of Poland's population. Today, as this synagogue in Warsaw bears witness, only a few remain. (Leo Erken/Impact Visuals)

But after more than half a century, the Holocaust continues to cause friction between Polish Catholics and Jews. Because so many Polish Catholics—1.5 million—died at Auschwitz, along with 2.5 million Jews, some Catholic Poles have resented the Jews claiming the Holocaust as exclusively theirs. For one American Jewish scholar, the roots of the resentment run far deeper than that. "Poland sees itself as the Christ of nations," said Lucy S. Dawidowicz. "There is a sense among the Poles that the Jews are usurping Polish suffering."[2]

This conflict came to a head in 1989, when Jewish Holocaust survivors urged the Catholic Church to remove a convent from the grounds of Auschwitz, claiming it was sacrilegious to their religion and suffering. The church vowed to remove the convent and then reneged on the promise. When a prominent Holocaust survivor denounced the church for its actions, conservative Polish Catholics urged the church not to give in to Jewish demands. This caused Primate Cardinal Jozef Glemp, the successor to Cardinal Wyszynski, to actually blame the "beloved Jews" for some of their own suffering. The convent was finally moved, but the incident has not been forgotten by either group.

Other Religious Groups

Catholicism and Judaism are not the only religions represented in Poland today. There are a small minority of Protestants and members of the Eastern Orthodox Church. But the most interesting religious minority by far is the Polish National Catholic Church. This sect is made up of Poles who broke away from the Roman Catholic Church in the United States in 1897 in response to the church's poor record in Polish-American communities. Although Polish Catholics were contributing their energies and money to the church, there were, at the time, few Polish priests and no Polish bishops in the United States. The Polish National Catholic Church of America remains the only major dissent group to break away from the Roman Catholic Church in the United States.

Missionaries from the new church first came to Poland in 1919. Twenty years later, there were over 50 parishes in Poland and a theological seminary in Kraków. In recent years, the PNCCA has entered into talks with the Roman Catholic Church in Poland.

Pope John Paul II

(1920–)

He is the world's most famous Pole, although he lives in Rome's Vatican City, hundreds of miles from his homeland. He is the first pope to come from a Communist country and probably the last. His intellect, fervent faith, and ceaseless energy have been an inspiration to millions of Catholics and non-Catholics the world over.

Pope John Paul II was born Karol Wojtyla near Kraków in Wadowice. His father was an officer in the Polish army and his mother a Lithuanian. He was an outstanding scholar and athlete in school and popular with the girls. As a young man, he divided his time between working in a chemical factory and acting in amateur theatricals. His first passion was not the church, but the theater.

For all his athletic vigor, he nearly died twice before becoming a priest. He was knocked down by a streetcar, and a short time later was run over by a truck. The first accident left him with a fractured skull; the second, permanently stooped shoulders.

During the Nazi occupation, Wojtyla began studying for the priesthood in an underground seminary in Kraków and was ordained in 1946. A scholarly cleric with a keen intellect, he balanced the responsibilities of a parish priest with the teaching duties at the Catholic University of Lublin and later the University of Kraków, and, in 1964, was made archbishop of that city.

Fluent in five languages, including Latin, Karol Cardinal Wojtyla learned English in preparation for his first visit to the United States in 1969. In the 1970s, he spoke out strongly against the Communist bureaucracy and was persecuted. In 1978, he became pope and became a staunch defender of traditional church values. He traveled around the world to speak out against such issues as divorce, birth control, and women priests, although he also spoke out for freedom from communism, poverty, and political repression.

In 1981, this beloved pope was shot and wounded outside St. Peter's Church in the Vatican by a Turkish terrorist. He forgave his attacker, who later personally confessed his sin to him. His three visits to his native land in 1979, 1983, and 1988 have inspired the Polish people and put continual pressure on the Communists to allow more freedom. Pope John Paul helped mediate the talks between the Communists and Solidarity that led to the fall of communism in Poland in 1989.

In the new, free Poland, the pope remains a more inspiring leader than any politician, although his unyielding conservative stand on some issues is being questioned even by Polish Catholics.

In his best-selling book, *Crossing the Threshold of Hope* (1994), he describes himself as a "man of joy and a man of hope, a man of the fundamental affirmation of the value of existence, the value of creation and of hope in the future life."[3]

Author, playwright, scholar, and head of the Roman Catholic Church—Pope John Paul II is one of the most popular popes of the 20th century. He is also the most widely traveled pope in history.
(The Bettmann Archive)

The Church in Poland Today

Religion continues to be an important factor in the new Poland. However, the Catholic Church, once the defender of the people, has lost a little of its luster now that communism has collapsed. As Western democratic ways have made inroads into Polish life, traditional values and the role of the church in Polish life are beginning to be questioned, as they are in other Eastern European countries.

The church is no longer accepted as the single authority on social issues. The Democratic Union's support of the church's strict stand against abortion and for Catholic education in public schools was a contributing factor in their losing the election of 1992. The former Communists of the Democratic Left Alliance, who supported abortion rights for Polish women, were voted into office.

In a 1993 survey conducted by the Institute of Public Opinion Studies, close to 60 percent of participants were opposed to the legislation of Christian moral values. However, despite signs that the church is losing ground, religion continues to be an important part of Polish life and will probably remain so as long as there is a Poland. As one 37-year-old pilgrim to Czestochowa said to a reporter in 1994, "Poland would not be Poland if it were not for the church."[4]

NOTES

1. Norman Davies, *God's Playground: A History of Poland*, Vol. II (New York: Columbia University Press, 1982), pp. 207–208.
2. *Newsweek*, September 11, 1989.
3. *The New York Times*, October 20, 1994.
4. *The New York Times*, August 30, 1994.

7

The Economy

When the *New York Times* conducted a poll in Eastern Europe in the summer of 1994, they asked a sampling of the Polish people what they felt about their country's economic future over the next five years. Some 28 percent of those asked believed the situation would stay about the same, 30 percent expected more deterioration in the economy, while only 41 percent believed their economic condition would improve.

With all this uncertainty, you'd think Poland was in dire economic straits, yet the truth is that by some measures the Polish economy is the most robust in Europe. In 1993, Poland enjoyed the fastest growth of any economy on the continent. Its gross national product grew an estimated 4 percent in 1993, while the other Eastern European countries lagged far behind.

So why are the Poles so skeptical about the future? The answer is a simple one. The same economic reform that has stimulated the economy and moved it steadily in the direction of a free-market economy has created stringent conditions for the average Pole. Under communism, 90 percent of all businesses were owned and run by the state. Unemployment was unheard of. Everybody worked. The standard of living was generally low and wages were meager, but at least a steady job and a living wage were guaranteed. With the move toward a free-market economy like that of the Western nations, the state no longer ran the country's businesses. Businesses were in the hands of individuals who competed for customers, and the law of the land has become survival of the fittest. After 40 years of Communistic paternalism, this new order is difficult for many Poles to adapt to in so short a time.

"I used to be paid for eight hours of work every day, no matter how much time I actually spent working," said a 43-year-old steel worker at the Huta Steelworks outside Warsaw. "Now, I work every minute I'm in the plant . . . What I'm worried about is that if the steel industry as a whole does badly, I could find myself laid off no matter how efficiently I work."[1]

That concern is justified. Since the fall of communism in 1989, the unemployment rate has zoomed from near zero to 16 percent in 1994, the highest in Eastern Europe. As state-run businesses are shutting down and small private businesses take over, inevitably companies will downsize to become profitable, like the steel industry already has. Jobs will continue to be lost.

On the other hand, as the economy grows and adjusts to the capitalistic system, new jobs will be created and, it is hoped, unemployment will drop substantially. However, it is difficult for Poles, like many peoples in Eastern Europe, to accept ongoing sacrifices today for a better tomorrow.

The Economy Under the Communists

Before looking closer at where the Polish economy is headed, it might do well to see where it's been. Before the Communists took control of the country, Poland was largely an agricultural society. Before the rebirth of the country after World War I, 60 percent of all Polish workers were farmers or agricultural laborers. Farms were small and far from productive.

Poor soil and harsh winters made, and still make, farming a hard vocation. Many farming families subsisted on the potatoes, barley, and beets they grew and had little or nothing to sell as surplus. The Communists tried to force collectivization on the Polish farmers as they did in the Soviet Union. Large, state-run farms were meant to replace small, private ones. However, the stubborn, independent Polish farmers refused to give up the little they had. By the early 1950s, the government gave up on trying to change them and by 1986, in the last days of communism, 85 percent of all Polish farms were privately owned.

But the economy had changed. The Communists promoted industry to modernize the country and built up vast factories and industrial centers around such cities as Warsaw and Kraków. They stressed the production of capital goods—heavy machinery and factory equipment—over consumer goods—clothing, furniture, appliances, and cars for the people. Furthermore, much of what was being manufactured in Poland, was being shipped out of the country to the Soviet Union. Polish goods were not benefiting the Polish people, but the Russians. Novelist James Michener recalls this phenomenon in his travels in Communist Poland:

> Wherever I had gone in those days it was the same. In Tarnow, boxcars carried farm produce into Russia. In Katowice, which I knew well from my visits, flatcars carried all the steel girders produced in the great Nowa Huta plants into Russia. In Gdansk, the fine new ships sailed to Russian home ports. Sometimes it seemed that nothing Polish produced remained at home.[2]

However greedy the Soviets were, they did allow a certain amount of free enterprise in Poland. While the government ran 90 percent of all industry, the remaining 10 percent was owned by individuals and cooperative groups. This relatively high rate of private business, compared to the other Eastern Bloc countries, was one important asset to the economy when communism fell in 1989. Since then, more than 1.6 million new businesses have appeared in Poland. Some have failed due to a weak banking system and a limited amount of liquid assets, but a surprising number have succeeded, further boosting the economy.

Small Businesses

Some of those businesses started under communism and now are flourishing under capitalism. Marek Postala, an engineering professor in Kraków, began a modest carpentry workshop some years ago. In 1992, his building and furniture company brought in $500,000 in sales. Malgorzata Zurawska, a linguist, made $3 million in sales last year from her chain of designer fashion stores in six cities. "The Polish people are intrinsically much stronger in business than outsiders thought,"[3] reported Ian Hume, the representative for the World Bank in Warsaw.

But for every success story there are many failures. The vast majority of Poles have not yet reaped the benefits of the free-market system. People who have lived their lives in uniform grimness now see their neighbors driving imported sports cars and living in big homes. This has created frustration and anger for many and caused some Poles to long for a simpler, if more repressive, time.

Foreign Trade

The promise of help from the Western nations to supply money and expertise to facilitate the changeover from one economy to another has largely gone unfulfilled. The European Union, a group of Western nations who joined together for trade, does business now with Poland and has even replaced Russia as its biggest foreign customer. However, it sells more imports to the Poles than it buys in exports. One obstacle to foreign trade with the European Union countries is high tariffs and taxes put on incoming Polish goods to help protect local industry.

"If you compare the current situation with our expectations in 1989–90, I will say we are not satisfied, because we thought things would go faster," said Polish Finance Minister Andrzej Olechowski. "If you press politicians in the West, they say yes, you can join us, at the turn of the century, but there is no agreement on a calendar to get there. Perhaps we were naive."[4] Some foreign businesses that have come to Poland have experienced their own set of frustrations. Gerber, the American baby-food company, established a factory in Poland, but found Polish mothers would not buy

Farming has never been easy in Poland's difficult climate, but it is still a major part of the economy. Potatoes, like these sold at this farmers' market in Poznan, are a major crop. (Rick Gerharter/Impact Visuals)

their products, preferring old family recipes to the manufactured Gerber food. In the larger cities, consumers were familiar with Gerber and its reputation, but found their prices too high. Gerber struggles on to find its share of the baby-food market, but its experience has led other American companies to think twice before opening operations in Poland.

Poland's Natural Resources

While industry struggles to provide the consumer goods people want, Poland's natural resources are another area of vast untapped potential.

Forests cover one-fourth of the country, but they have not been exploited to any great extent. While natural gas and petroleum deposits are more limited, they have not been exploited and 35 percent of Poland's fuel comes from other countries, most notably Russia.

Since communism's collapse, many foreign manufacturers have entered Poland's new consumer society. Here, shoppers wait patiently for a chance to view the wares in a Levi's store in Poznan. (Rick Gerharter/Impact Visuals)

One resource that has been used well is coal. Poland is the sixth largest coal-mining country and produced 213 million tons (215 million metric tons) of coal in 1990. The coalfield around the city of Katowice is one of the largest in the world. Poland also has smaller amounts of copper, lead, zinc, sulfur, and salt.

Agriculture, despite the many difficulties of raising crops, is also big business in Poland. It is the second largest producer of rye and potatoes in the world, after Russia. Barley, sugar beets, wheat, alfalfa, and clover are also important crops. Some grains are used to make Polish vodka, one of the most prized vodkas in the world. Livestock makes up two-fifths of total agricultural production. Hogs are raised throughout the country for processing as ham, sausage, and bacon. Sheep and cattle are raised for meat, wool, and milk in the grassy hills of the south.

Poland's new former Communist leaders claim to have no intention of halting the march to a free-market economy. They say for Poland there is no other road to prosperity. They have only tempered the zeal of the conservatives and centrists by slowing down reform. If they hope to remain in power, they will have to carefully balance the needs of the nation with the current dissatisfaction of the poor and dispossessed.

While the pains and anguish of many have not disappeared, the future is looking better. In March 1994, after four years of seemingly endless negotiations, Poland's huge international debt, which stood at more than $4.5 billion to the United States alone in 1990, was reduced by over 40 percent by Western commercial banks. The reduction in debt, too, should further stimulate an economy that is already among the strongest in Eastern Europe. Polish perseverance, an age-old characteristic that has kept the Poles in good stead so many times in the past, may well set them on the path to a bright economic future.

NOTES

1. *The New York Times*, April 30, 1994.
2. James Michener, *Pilgrimage: A Memoir of Poland and Rome* (Emmaus, Pa.: Rodale Press, 1990), pp. 20–21.
3. *The New York Times*, June 20, 1993.
4. *The New York Times*, April 30, 1994.

8

Culture

*T*he coming of Christianity to Poland in A.D. 966 did much more than make Poland a Catholic country. It also made it, despite its location in the heart of Eastern Europe, very much a Western nation. Along with priests and missionaries, the pope in Rome sent artists and scholars from the center of Western Europe to Poland. These people spread Western views and styles that had a profound effect on Polish architecture, literature, art, music, science, law, and education.

Because of their vulnerability to enemies, Poles have cultivated a strong sense of patriotism and national pride over the centuries. Polish culture, particularly its literature and art, have followed suit. The most characteristic works of Poland's finest artists and writers until recently reflected national concerns and themes more than personal and individual ones. Poland's creative minds have traditionally tended to look more outward than inward.

Language

Among European languages, Polish is one of the most formidable-looking to nonspeakers with its strange combinations of consonants and vowels. A Slavic language, similar to Russian, Polish has 10 vowels and 35 consonants. It has been enriched over the centuries with vocabulary from German, Italian, French, English, and Ukrainian. Polish is spoken by more than 38 million people in the world today, including about 3 million in the United States.

Literature

The first great flowering of Polish literature and the other arts was in the 16th century under the Jagiellonian kings during the nation's golden age. It perhaps reached its pinnacle in the poetry of Jan Kochanowski (1530–84). This versatile writer adapted the poetic traditions of France and Italy and fashioned from them a poetic language that raised Polish literature to new heights. His poems cover an extraordinary range of subjects and moods, from stirring patriotic lyrics to sorrowful elegies to his dead daughter. Kochanowski even wrote a Polish version of the Bible's Book of Psalms.

The second golden age of Polish literature came not when Poland was at the height of greatness but at its nadir. During the 19th century, when Poland had ceased to exist as a nation, poets and novelists kept the flame of Polish nationalism alive in epic novels and poems about the greatness of their country's past. Henryk Sienkiewicz (1846–1916), who became the first Polish writer to win the Nobel Prize for literature in 1905, wrote a trilogy about Poland's struggle against invaders in the 17th century. Poet Adam Mickiewicz (1798–1855) symbolized Poland's fight with Russia in his epic poem *Kamad Wallenrad* about the earlier wars with the Teutonic Knights. An exile for much of his adult life, Mickiewicz was arrested and exiled by the Russians for "spreading wrong-headed Polish nationalism" through his early poems and political activities.

Another great Polish writer who wrote movingly of Poland's poor and underprivileged was Waldyslaw Stanislaw Reymont (1867–1926). Born into grinding poverty in a peasant village, Reymont escaped into a make-believe world of theater when he joined a troupe of traveling actors. This experience served as the basis for his first novel, *The Comedienne* (1896). His masterpiece is his four-volume epic *The Peasants* (1902–09) that shows the heroic character of Poland's simple villagers. For this and other works, Reymont became the second Pole, after Sienkiewicz, to win a Nobel Prize in literature in 1924.

With the rebirth of Poland in 1919, a group of urban poets, who called themselves the Skamander group, encouraged Polish writers to look inward and abandon traditional forms for more experimental ones. This new movement was short-lived, however. The German occupation of World War II dealt a terrible blow to Polish culture and the arts. The nightmarish war years were poignantly captured in the terse, concentration camp stories of Tadeusz Borowski (1922–51). At age 21, Borowski was imprisoned in Auschwitz and Dachau for two years. In *This Way for the Gas, Ladies and Gentlemen*, Borowski describes the arrival of a trainload of doomed Jews at his camp:

The bolts crack, the doors fall open. A wave of fresh air rushes inside the train. People . . . inhumanly crammed, buried under incredible heaps of luggage, suitcases, trunks, packages, crates, bundles of every description (everything that had been their past and was to start their future). Monstrously squeezed together, they have fainted from heat, suffocated, crushed one another. Now they push towards the opened doors, breathing like fish cast out on the sand. . . .

A huge, multicolored wave of people loaded down with luggage, pours from the train like a blind, mad river trying to find a new bed. But before they have a chance to recover, before they can draw a breath of fresh air and look at the sky, bundles are snatched from their hands, coats ripped off their backs, their purses and umbrella taken away. . . .

The heaps grow. Suitcases, bundles, blankets, coats, handbags that open as they fall, spilling coins, gold, watches; mountains of bread pile up at the exits, heaps of marmalade, jams, masses of meat, sausages; sugar spills on the gravel. Trucks, loaded with people, start up with a deafening roar and drive off amidst the wailing and screaming of the women separated from their children, and the stupefied silence of the men left behind. They are the ones who had been ordered to step to the right—the healthy and the young who

Frédéric Chopin

(1810–1849)

He was not a great performer, he never mastered the classical form of the symphony, and he died of tuberculosis before he was 40. But no classical composer of the 19th century was a greater master of piano composition than Frédéric Chopin.

Chopin was born in Zelazona-Wola, near Warsaw, to a French father and a Polish mother. He was a child prodigy and wrote his first composition, a polonaise—a kind of stately Polish dance—at age seven. He gave his first public concert the following year. After graduating from the Warsaw Conservatory, Chopin traveled abroad and settled in Paris in 1831. Too sickly to perform much, he earned a living teaching wealthy women the piano while composing. Although he wrote sonatas, waltzes, and two piano concertos, Chopin's best known and most loved compositions are his 40 mazurkas, Polish folk dances, and 15 polonaises. These pieces burst with national pride and a deep love for his native land, which he never saw again after the age of 20.

In 1837, Chopin met and fell in love with Aurore Dupin, the novelist better known to the world by her pseudonym George Sand. They were an unlikely match—the strong, masculine Sand who liked to scandalize society by smoking cigars in public, and the weak, refined Chopin. However, their relationship lasted nine years, and Sand was the great love of

will go to the camp. In the end, they too will not escape death, but first they must work.

Trucks leave and return, without interruption, as on a monstrous conveyor belt. A Red Cross van drives back and forth, back and forth, incessantly: it transports the gas that will kill these people. The enormous cross on the hood, red as blood, seems to dissolve in the sun.[1]

Borowski survived the death camps but they haunted him the rest of his life. Disillusioned with the new Communist regime that turned him into a propagandist hack, Borowski committed suicide by gas asphyxiation three day after his wife, who survived the camps with him, gave birth to their daughter.

Chopin's life. Her tender care and attention helped him conserve his energies for composing many of his finest works. When they separated in 1846, Chopin's health declined and he all but gave up composing.

Chopin left France for England two years later and briefly revived his career on the concert stage. He even gave a private performance for Queen Victoria. One of his last concerts was fittingly a benefit for Polish refugees. He died in Paris of tuberculosis, the disease that had haunted him for years, on October 17, 1849. A year later, a monument of a weeping Muse with a broken lyre was erected over his grave. When it was dedicated, a tiny box of Polish soil was sprinkled on the grave. The exile had come home at last.

The sensitive nature of Frédéric Chopin is captured in this drawing by novelist George Sand, the woman who was the great love of his life.
(The New York Public Library Picture Collection)

Five years later, a thaw in the Communist regime allowed a certain amount of creative freedom to writers and intellectuals, although that freedom had its limits. Some of the best contemporary writers during the Communist era chose to turn away from realism toward fantasy and satire in order to criticize the Communist system indirectly. In his satirical plays and fablelike stories, Slawomir Mrozek (1936–) savaged the Communists and their bureaucracy in a comic and entertaining style. Another writer, Stanislaw Lem (1921–), turned to surrealistic science fiction to escape the grimness of Communist Poland. Czeslaw Milosz (1911–) is Poland's most celebrated contemporary poet, but he is best known in the West for his essay "The Captive Mind," a stinging critique of communism. Milosz won the Nobel Prize for literature in 1980. By their sharp-edged humor, humanity, and courage, these writers and other Polish intellectuals fought the Communist system, and eventually contributed to its downfall.

Music

While literature was an inspiration for 19th-century Poles, it was in the stirring polonaises and murzakas of Frédéric Chopin (see boxed biography) that Polish patriotism was best expressed for the rest of the Western world. While Chopin's exquisite piano works reflect his deep love of his homeland, many of his other compositions, particularly his études, reflect deeply personal feelings that looked forward to the modernism of the 20th century.

Polish classical music in the 20th century has more directly mirrored the violence and political upheavals that the country has experienced. Poland's best known modern composer, Krzystof Penderecki (1933–), has written the stirring *Threnody for the Victims of Hiroshima* (1960), a tribute from a Polish war survivor to other victims of that war half a world away. A restless innovator, Penderecki has incorporated typewriting, sawing wood, and hissing singers in his works.

Witold Lutoslawski (1913–94) used elements of Polish folk music in his work and won a Grammy in the United States in 1986 for a recording of his Symphony No. 3. Henryk Gorecki (1933–), another popular composer, wrote his *Miserere* to commemorate the police violence against Solidarity in 1981 and paid musical tribute to the pope's third visit to his homeland in 1987 in his *Totus Tues.*

Art

Polish visual artists have not often shared in the international fame of their compatriot writers and composers. The first Polish painter to have a world-wide reputation was Jean Matejko (1838–93). What Mickiewicz and Sienkiewicz achieved in literature, Matejko realized in his huge historical paintings, which depict some of the finest moments in Polish history.

Here is how one French critic described Matejko's work:

> [they are] enormous canvases, fifteen or twenty feet long, encumbered with people in diverse costumes, full of bizarre details, spotted with brilliant colors, which are piled one on the other so that the air and the light cannot play between them. At first the eye suffers from this tumult, then one discovers an original composition, great firmness of drawing, energetic and free attitudes, and figures of surprising rudeness.[2]

Polish artists in the 20th century turned away from the grandeur of epic painting to the more contained but equally propagandic art of the poster. Chief among these poster artists is Franciszek Starowicyski whose weird fantastic art includes the repeated imagery of disembodied eyeballs, spiders, and skulls. Starowicyski's work, according to one art review in the *New York Times*, "catches a sense of nonrelieved gloom that might easily be seen to reflect a repressive society that wasn't working very well."[3]

The most exciting development in the Polish art world since the fall of communism is the opening in 1990 of the Center for Contemporary Art, located in 17th-century Ujozdowski Castle.

"This museum is a kind of laboratory of the arts; it is a space for art in progress,"[4] said its director and Solidarity supporter Wojociech Krukowski. Shows such as a comparison of Stalinist Social Realism paintings with huge Polish installation art of the 1980s, has given the museum an international reputation. Unfortunately, the minister of culture in the new government is not a modern art enthusiast and has cut back government funding for the museum. Whether the museum can survive will depend largely on the support of the Polish people and foreign art lovers.

Film and Theater

Polish filmmakers have also had a strong interest in the macabre and the gruesome. Perhaps none more so than French-born Polish director Roman Polanski (1933–). Polanski, who was born Jewish, had a horrible childhood in war-torn Poland. His parents were taken to a concentration

Andrzej Wajda

(1926–)

Few 20th-century artists have plumbed the depths of the Polish national character as deeply and passionately as filmmaker Andrzej Wajda. Poland's most distinguished director for four decades, his films wrestle with the forces that have both inspired and ravaged his nation.

Poland's most celebrated film director, Andrzej Wajda is also a national hero. Such overtly political films as his Man of Marble *and* Man of Iron, *made during the Communist era, would probably have been censored if any other filmmaker had made them.*
(The Bettmann Archive)

camp when he was eight, and he wandered the countryside finding shelter from the storm with a series of Catholic families. After the war, Polanski studied film at the famous Polish Film School at Lodz, where most of Poland's best directors got their start. After making several surreal shorts and a superb psychological thriller, *Knife in the Water* (1962), Polanski left Poland and eventually came to Hollywood where he made such classic horror and crime films as *Rosemary's Baby* (1968) and *Chinatown* (1974). In 1981, Polanski returned to Poland and directed and starred in Peter Shaffer's play *Amadeus* in Warsaw.

While veteran directors like Andrzej Wajda (see boxed biography) continue to probe Poland's past and present in political dramas and war films, younger directors like Wladyslaw Pasikowski, are moving in other

Wajda's father was a cavalry officer who died on the battlefield in World War II. At 16, Wajda became a Resistance fighter against the Nazis who occupied his country. When Poland was liberated after the war, he became an art student at the Krakow Academy of Fine Arts and later enrolled in the famous Lodz film school. After graduating in 1952, he worked as an assistant to Polish filmmaker Aleksander Ford, director of Film Polski, the government-run film organization.

Wajda's first film *A Generation* (1954), dealt with Polish youth resistance during the Nazi occupation and was largely based on his own experiences. It proved to be the first part of a memorable war trilogy. *Kanal* (1957) told in gripping detail the story of a group of Resistance fighters during the Warsaw Uprising, trying to escape through the city's underground sewers. *Ashes and Diamonds* (1958) was even more searing, as a doomed Polish nationalist struggles with his last assignment—the assassination of a leading bureaucrat who has sold out to the Communists in postwar Poland. Wajda boldly set the final death scene of the assassin, played by Zbigniew Cybulski, the Polish James Dean, against lines of white laundry and heaps of rubble.

Wajda's subsequent films have ranged from pointed comedies to historical films to contemporary political dramas. His best films have looked unflinchingly at the futility of war and the waste of heroism. For all his bitter cynicism, Wajda has never given up hope for the future of his country. When the first freely elected Polish parliament took office in 1989, among its most celebrated members was the filmmaker Andrzej Wajda.

directions. His action thriller *Dogs 2* (1993) about a Pole's involvement with the Russian Mafia, is one of the biggest box-office hits in post-Communist Poland.

"When someone says my movies are Hollywoodish, I consider that a great compliment," says Pasikowski. "My role is not to preach, just to tell a story."[5]

One of the most influential and innovative artists in the Polish theater is Jerzy Grotowski (1933–), founder and director of the Wroclaw Laboratory Theater. Grotowski's "poor theater" reduces play performance to the absolute essentials, doing away with costumes, makeup, lighting, and sound effects.

Folk Art and Music

There is a side to Polish culture that does not stem from individual artists and writers but from the common people. While the cities have largely lost touch with the folk art and music of Poland, both still flourish in the villages and small towns of the countryside. The Kurpianka Cepelia Cooperative was established in 1950 to encourage folk artists to make and sell their tapestries, wood carvings, pottery, and other folk art pieces at specialty shops called Cepelia stores. The Cooperative also supports village musicians in the Green Forest song and dance ensemble. Other folk festivals keep this very lively but complicated music alive from the Tatra region to Kaimierz, a town on the banks of the Vistula River.

This paper cut of flowers from Lowicz in central Poland is a stunning example of Polish folk art. Folk art is sold throughout the country in specialty shops called Cepelia stores. (The Polish National Tourist Office in New York/Z. Zyburlowice)

As Poland enters a new era of freedom, old problems and issues will give way to new ones. These will be examined and reflected in Polish culture, a culture that has been a comfort and a support to its people in both good times and bad.

NOTES

1. Tadeusz Borowski, *This Way for the Gas, Ladies and Gentlemen* (New York: Penguin, 1976), pp. 37–38.
2. Quoted in *Artists of the 19th Century and Their Works* (Boston: Houghton Mifflin, 1899), p. 99.
3. *The New York Times*, May 16, 1993.
4. *The New York Times*, September 19, 1994.
5. *The New York Times*, April 30, 1994.

9

Daily Life

Daily life in Poland is not easy. Under communism, Poles were deprived of the most basic consumer goods and comforts. Now, caught between a planned economy that never worked and a free-market one that is still evolving, Poland's standard of living remains low compared to the United States and most countries in Western Europe. The fervent complaint of Halina Bortnowska, a lay Catholic activist from Kraków, echoes the feelings of millions of ordinary Poles:

> We live from one day to the next, and we've been doing it for too long—for years now—and we're tired, we're exhausted. Every morning, I wake up and wonder, Is my washing machine going to work today? . . . on that day [that it doesn't] my standard of living will take a decisive plunge. Because I'll never be able to afford a new one, not ever again. . . . And every day, waking up, I wonder, Is this going to be the day? *About everything*. And this is no way to live.[1]

Another woman, Joanna Jedraszkiewicz, who lost her job as a graphic designer, was even more pessimistic. "I am 50 and have no future. What are they going to do with my generation? Shoot them?"[2]

Despite these problems, most Poles, as they have so many times in the past, keep their faith and try to look forward to a better future. In the meantime, they continue to work hard, play hard, and wait.

Housing

Housing has been a problem in Poland for decades and has only gradually improved since communism's fall. As masses of people have over the years moved from the country to the towns and cities to work in industry, finding adequate housing for them has been a constant problem. Further aggravated by a high birthrate, the housing shortage has, in the last few decades, reached epidemic proportions in some cities.

Many families live in two-room apartments with everyone sleeping in the same bedroom. Thousands of people are on waiting lists for new apartments. Some wait as long as five years just to get an apartment that they don't have to share with relatives or another family.

Education

Education is important in Poland and always has been. With the collapse of communism, Marxist indoctrination has ended in schools and opened the door to a free exchange of ideas. Elementary school—from ages 7 to 15—is compulsory in Poland. Secondary school, roughly the equivalent of American high school, begins at age 16 and runs four years. In secondary school, the workload increases and students are expected to choose a special field of study, much as American students do in college. Both elementary and secondary students must attend a half day of school on Saturdays. Education is free up to the university level.

There are a number of other differences in the way schools are run in Poland as compared to those in the United States. When students enter their classroom, for instance, they remove their shoes in the cloakroom

Those students who do not enter a university may learn a trade in a Polish technical school. These students at Torun's School of Gastronomy are making a dish as part of their "final exam." (Connie Grosch/Impact Visuals)

and put on special slippers they will wear all day at school. These help to keep the school's floors clean. Although most elementary students take six subjects, including a foreign language, they remain in one classroom all day. The teachers are the ones who go from room to room each period.

Teachers are strict and class procedure is more formal than in most American schools. If a student does something bad or breaks a rule, it is announced publicly to the entire student body. The shame and embarrassment the student experiences will hopefully prevent him or her from misbehaving again.

Those students who do well academically in secondary school and pass the stringent entrance exams, go on to study at one of Poland's 10 universities or one of the specialized schools in music or theater. Those students who do not make the grade or have no interest in higher education have several options. They can go to work, join the armed services, or apply to one of Poland's many technical schools.

Sexual Issues

Sexuality was largely repressed under communism and while the Catholic Church still wields influence it is not being listened to as dutifully on such matters as abortion and sex outside of marriage as it once was. Traditional family values have prevented Polish women from having a strong individual identity in the past, but, in the freer 1990s, this too is changing. "Slowly there has started to be a feminist movement here," leading Polish stage and screen actress Krystyna Janda has said. "Then recently you could see it on television, in books, at conferences. Awareness rose very quickly and it seemed women wanted to make up for lost time."[3]

This new assertiveness of Polish women, has had its price. Some husbands have left their wives, leading psychologists to write magazine articles telling women how to cope with these new and unexpected situations.

Sports and Recreation

Soccer is Poland's most popular sport and it is played in every school. Professional soccer is Poland's most popular spectator sport, and crowds flock to the giant sports stadium in Warsaw and in other cities to see teams in Poland's two pro divisions play. Volleyball and basketball are other popular team sports, while gymnastics, swimming, and ice skating are the favorite individual sports. Table tennis and tennis have also become popular with young people in recent years.

Most Poles enjoy the outdoors. During summer vacation, many city families travel south to the Tatra Mountains, a popular vacation area. They spend their time enjoying nature, which they don't get to see much of the rest of the year. They go on hikes, canoe and swim. To get out of the city, many young people hitchhike. Poland is one of the few Western countries where hitchhiking is not only legal, but encouraged by the government. A hitchhiking committee issues coupon books to hitchhikers. When a driver picks him or her up, the hitchhiker gives the person coupons from the book. At the end of the year, those drivers with the highest number of coupons are awarded prizes.

Food

Eating is a serious business in Poland. Polish cuisine is one of the best kept secrets in Europe. Each conquering group dominating Poland brought dishes from home, which the Poles adapted to their own cuisine.

Polish weddings are a time for celebrating. The grandfather of the bride accepts a glass of vodka, the national drink, at this wedding party. (Connie Grosch/ Impact Visuals)

This blending of cuisines has made Polish cooking one of the most interesting and original in the world. Americans, even those of Polish descent, who think Polish food begins and ends with the sausage kielbasa and stuffed dumplings called pierogis, may be surprised to learn the great range and variety of Polish food.

Polish families gather around the dining table for their biggest meal of the day, *obiad*, or dinner. Many families share this meal most nights around 5:00 P.M., but some eat as early as 3:00 or 4:00 P.M., depending on their work schedules.

Polish dinners often begin with a bowl of soup. Poles love homemade soup and make an astounding variety of it. A national favorite is *barszcz*, or beet soup. It consists of pork and beef stock, diced pickled beets, and dried mushrooms, with a generous dollop of sour cream, a favorite garnish, on top. In the hot summer months, Poles relish cold soups made from native fruits.

Soup is followed by the main dish—beef, ham, or perhaps baked fish. Fish may seem an odd entrée in a largely landlocked country, but Poland's many lakes abound with carp, pike, and cod, while herring comes from the chilly Baltic Sea. The fish is cooked in a mushroom sauce. Mushrooms grow wild in many parts of Poland and picking them is a favorite family activity. Along with the main course are boiled potatoes and perhaps stuffed tomatoes. Dinner ends with a rich dessert such as *naleszniki*, thin pancakes stuffed with fruit.

The Media

Poland's more than 80 newspapers have flourished in the wake of communism. Once mere mouthpieces of the government and forced to follow the party line, journalists have taken to honest, investigative work with a vengeance. They have exposed the corruption and other crimes of the new Polish politicians and alerted the public to threatened encroachments on personal freedoms from former Communists in power.

Polish television has come a long way since the dreary days of communism. There are still two state channels, but the introduction of cable TV has brought a far greater variety of programming. With 1.2 million cable customers, Poland is the seventh largest cable user in Europe today.

Polish youth enjoy MTV, while their parents favor such shows as "Kolo Fortuna," the Polish version of the American game show "Wheel of Fortune."

Holidays

While daily life can be a grind for many Poles, there are a number of holidays throughout the year that offer them a chance to relax and celebrate.

The two biggest holidays in Poland are Christmas and Easter. Christmas is more than a holiday to the Poles, it is an entire season that begins on St. Martin's Day, November 12, and continues until Twelfth Night on January 6. The nearly two months between these two dates are filled with religious services, feasting, celebrating, and gift giving.

Roast goose is the traditional fare on St. Martin's Day, while St. Andrew's Day (November 30), resembles an autumnal St. Valentine's Day. Young men and women wear cherry blossoms on this day and bestow them on their sweethearts. According to another folk tradition, young people put a twig from a cherry tree into a cup of water. If the twig blooms before the new year, they will find romance and happiness in the coming year.

St. Nicholas Day, December 6, is the traditional day of gift giving, as it is in many European countries. Children receive religious pictures, presents, and pastries. As Christmas draws nearer, the households become filled with the smell of *pierniki*, honey cakes baked in the shape of animals and Nativity scenes. They are baked and stored away to be aged and eaten on Christmas Eve. While Christmas carolers traditionally entertain families in other countries during the Christmas season, in Poland, puppeteers go from house to house acting out the Nativity story for children and their parents in exchange for cookies and a cup of good cheer.

On Christmas Eve, the entire season reaches its culmination. Many Catholics fast all day in anticipation of the evening feast. Christmas Eve dinner, the *wigilia*, is traditionally meatless and includes baked fish, beet soup, potato dumplings, cabbage, and numerous rich desserts. Hearty appetites may have no qualms about overindulging, for it is bad luck not to taste every dish. After eating, the family sings Christmas carols and opens gifts. The memorable night ends with everyone attending midnight mass at the local church.

Christmas Day, as it is in many places, is a more quiet time spent with family and friends. Food is cooked in advance so no one has to work in the kitchen. A Christmas favorite is *bigos*, or hunter's stew, a savory blend of sausage, sauerkraut, pork, cabbage, and spices, that can take up to a week to cook.

New Year's Eve, known as Sylvester in Poland, is marked by parties and balls filled with music and dancing. Special almond cakes have coins baked inside them. Those who find a coin will have good luck in the new year.

Easter is a time of prayer and *pisanki*, Polish Easter eggs. These decorated eggs are something of a fine art with their rich designs and bold colors. They are used, along with flowers, to decorate the Easter table, which groans with ham, sausage, vegetables, soups, and wines. On Holy Saturday, the day before Easter Sunday, parishioners take decorated baskets of food to the local church to be blessed by the priest. A special Easter dish is butter made into the shape of a lamb, the symbol of Christ, with cloves for eyes, lying on a green bed of parsley.

Easter Monday, in sharp contrast to the previous day's solemnity, is a time of high spirits and romance—both signs of the coming of spring. Boys and men spray water or perfume on their sweethearts or wives. It is a good example of how pagan rites mingle with Christian ones on Polish holidays.

Life in Poland is full-bodied and hearty, like a rich Polish soup. Here, the ordinary and the extraordinary, the sacred and the profane, exist in the same simmering bowl.

NOTES

1. Lawrence Weschler, "Deficit," *The New Yorker*, May 11, 1992, p. 60.
2. *The New York Times*, September 18, 1993.
3. *The New York Times*, February 16, 1995.

10

The Cities

A nation's achievements and aspirations are often best reflected in its cities. The devastation and destruction that Poland experienced in World War II, under German occupation, nearly obliterated its cities and all they represented. City after city was burned, plundered, and razed by the Nazis.

Warsaw—The City That Wouldn't Die

No Polish metropolis suffered more in World War II than its largest city and capital, Warsaw. Ninety percent of the city's buildings were destroyed. Two-thirds of its population were killed or imprisoned. Centuries-old buildings were reduced to rubble and ash. By war's end, Warsaw was a burned shell of its former self.

A modern highway cuts through Warsaw's colorful Old Town. The Royal Castle can be seen on the right. (Polish National Tourist Office, New York)

The people of Warsaw might have been expected to start over and build modern high-rise apartments and office buildings on the sites of ancient churches and palaces. But anyone who thought that did not know the Poles' love of their great city. Using old photographs, pictures, and architectural designs and plans, they lovingly recreated an exact replica of Warsaw as it had been before the war. Today, Warsaw is a modern city that retains much of its old-world charm and dignity, thanks to the painstaking efforts of its residents.

Warsaw (pop. 1,655,000)* is situated in central Poland and is divided in two by the Vistula River. The river, according to legend, played a major role in the city's founding. A fisherman, so the story goes, was fishing on the banks of the Vistula when a mermaid appeared to him. The sea

---

*All populations given in this chapter are 1989 estimates.

creature told him that one day a great city would be built on the very spot where he stood. The fisherman, named Warsz, gave his name to the city, and the mermaid is still commemorated in the city's coat of arms.

The first record of the historical Warsaw appeared in the 900s when a small settlement inhabited by Slavic tribes was noted. A few hundred years later, Warsaw became the official residence of the dukes of Mazovia, a family of Polish nobles. In 1596 King Sigismund III moved his capital from Kraków to Warsaw when Mazovia became part of his kingdom.

As Poland's fortunes fell in the 17th century, so did Warsaw's. Swedish invaders destroyed much of the city in 1656. It ceased to be a capital when the Prussians took it over in the final partition of Poland in 1795. The city briefly emerged to become the capital of Napoleon's Duchy of Warsaw in 1807. Russia regained control of the territory six years later and relegated Warsaw to obscurity once again.

The city was, nevertheless, a hotbed of national resistance in the 19th century and was the scene of two aborted rebellions in 1830 and 1863. Control of Warsaw passed from Russia to Germany in World War I, ending in its independence in 1918. The Nazis lay siege to the city in 1939 and devastated it. Warsaw's residents surrendered, but never admitted defeat. Warsaw became the hub of the Polish Underground resistance.

In the war's final days, knowing they faced imminent defeat, the Nazis exacted their final revenge on the city. They burned and blew up those buildings that had eluded destruction in five years of conflict. The Soviets, who could have saved Warsaw from this last indignity, waited outside the city and only moved in to "liberate" it on January 17, 1945 when the Germans had finished. Today, memories of the war years can be seen everywhere. Statues, monuments, and memorials to the war dead dot the city. Most moving of all are the flower-laden plaques, marking the spots where Poles were killed during the war.

By February 1945, Warsaw was a capital city again, but not of a free nation. The Soviets had taken over and established the Communist Polish People's Republic.

To understand Warsaw, you must know its two sections, divided by the Vistula. To the west, on the right bank, is modern Warsaw, home to Polish industry and countless housing projects. Here factories manufacture electronic equipment, machinery, automobiles, and textiles. On the right bank is Warsaw's celebrated Old Town (*Stare Miasto*), which dates back to the 13th century. Its ancient buildings, twisting medieval streets and grand churches have been lovingly restored. To add to the charm of this medieval "town," the government has closed it off to motorized traffic. Couples stroll its streets on foot or in horse-drawn carriages. The Old Town marketplace is alive with outdoor art displays and cozy cafés called *karviarnie*, where students, artists, and writers sit and sip coffee, eat cake, and talk.

Nearby is the Royal Walk, a two-mile (3 km) route that stretches from Castle Square, site of Warsaw's Royal Castle, once the abode of Polish kings and presidents, to Lazienki Palace, whose park houses a monument to Poland's greatest composer, Frédéric Chopin. Concerts of Chopin's music are held in the park each summer, while every five years the city hosts the Chopin International Piano Competition. Chopin's home is another highlight on the Royal Walk. So are the Laboratory of Physical Sciences where Madame Curie once worked, the University of Warsaw, and the Botanical Gardens.

The new Warsaw, however, is not as comforting as the old. And it presents stark and disturbing contrasts to visitors, as this Polish-American writer observed:

> Stretch limousines carry the new rich through the streets. Ikea, the Swedish furniture chain, and Benetton, the Italian apparel outfit, have opened stores to sell them merchandise. . . . But while people earning $60 a week can buy books and, from time to time, a Benetton sweater for $30 . . . they can't afford much more. . . .
>
> Most Poles still live in run-down buildings whose piping breaks down regularly. Windowpanes in the doors of apartment buildings are broken, half covered with cardboard. This is not in slum territories but in respectable middle-class neighborhoods.[1]

Legendary Kraków

If Warsaw is Poland's Moscow, then Kraków (pop. 748,000) is surely its St. Petersburg. The third largest city of Poland, Kraków emerged from the catastrophe of World War II practically unscathed. Its age-old beauty entranced even the cold-hearted German Nazi commanders who decided to make it their headquarters. Thus its magnificent castles and cathedrals were spared the devastation of war.

Kraków was a thriving trade center when Warsaw was still a village. Here is how author Eric P. Kelly describes 15th-century Kraków in his historical novel, *The Trumpeter of Krakow*, as seen through the eyes of a Polish family entering the city for the first time:

> All about them rose in the bright sunlit palaces, churches, towers, battlement walls, and Gothic buildings, as yet for the most part unadorned by the rich sculpture that was to come in a few years under the influence of the Italian Renaissance. . . .
>
> Here for the moment in this great international capital of East and West was worshiped every god that man knows, it might even be said that God himself was worshiped under many names and in many languages and dialects. Here was Turks, Cossacks, Ruthenians, Germans, Flemings, Czechs, and Slovaks, with their wares to sell, and Hungarians with their wines from the mellow plains of Transylvania.[2]

A very different view of Kraków in the 1990s, emerging from 40 years of Communist neglect is offered by American correspondent for the *New York Times*, Jane Perlez:

> Cracow . . . is emerging again as a European city of charm and vibrancy. Many of the elegant small Gothic and Renaissance palaces that rim the main square have been repainted in the last two years. Jazz spots in stone cellars are being scrubbed down; new sidewalk cafés with spiffy furniture and umbrellas are opening almost weekly, it seems. . . .
>
> This reawakening is taking place against the backdrop of Cracow's immutable strengths: an old town of narrow cobbled streets and 60 churches . . .[3]

Perhaps the most prominent of these "strengths" is Wawel Hill, a natural limestone promontory that overlooks the banks of the Vistula in south central Poland. On it sits Wawel Castle and Cathedral. Legend has it, before either of these were built, there was a cave on the site, inhabited by a terrible dragon. The Wawel Dragon was the terror of the Polish countryside, burning homes and eating people and animals.

The king of the region offered a tempting reward to any knight who could slay the creature—the hand of his daughter in marriage and his

Wawel Castle, supposedly built above a cave where a legendary dragon lived, is one of Kraków's grandest sights. The equestrian statue is of Polish hero Tadeusz Kosciuzsko. (The Bettmann Archive)

kingdom to rule after his death. Many brave knights tried to vanquish the dragon, but all died in the attempt.

A shoemaker's apprentice named Krak decided to use his wits to defeat the monster. Krak stuffed a ram's skin with sulfur, sewed it up, and placed it before the dragon's cave. The hungry beast devoured the skin, and the sulfur caused the flame in its stomach to burn all the more intensely. The dragon became extremely thirsty and quaffed down water from the river until he was ready to burst. Krak began to tease the dragon, whose fire was quenched by the water and could now only spew out steam. The frustrated dragon puffed out more and more steam, until the pressure of the steam in his body caused him to explode. Krak won the princess and celebrated his good future by building a castle on top of the dragon's cave. He called it Wawel Castle after the unfortunate dragon and founded the city of Kraków, which grew up around the castle.

Wawel Cathedral is more firmly grounded in Polish history. It was built by Boleslaw the Brave in 1020 and later became the burial place of Polish kings and such national heroes as Tadeuz Koscuizsko and Josef Pilsudski. Here also lies the silver tomb of St. Stanislaus, Poland's patron saint.

Boleslaw's successors made Kraków the capital of Poland in 1038, and it remained the capital for over 500 years. The crown jewel of Poland's "golden age," Kraków is home to the nation's oldest university, the University of Kraków (now Jagiellonian University), built in 1364 by Casimir the Great and designed by Italian Renaissance architects. Among the most precious articles on display at the university are the astronomical tools of Copernicus, who studied there, and the world-famous Jagiellonian Globe, made in 1510 and the first to show the New World lands.

Another beguiling legend, this one based on fact, is connected with the Church of St. Mary. Seven hundred years ago the people of Kraków were celebrating in the church, when a watchman in the church tower saw an invading army of Tartars advancing in a surprise attack. The watchman immediately lifted his trumpet and played the "Heynal," a hymn to Our Lady and a signal of alarm. An approaching Tartar soldier shot the watchman in the throat with an arrow. The brave trumpeter died, having alerted the people of Kraków to the danger and thereby saving the city from destruction. In remembrance of this historical moment, a trumpeter plays the "Heynal" in the same church tower every hour of the day. When he comes to the high note, he breaks off, just as the original trumpeter did when pierced by the arrow.

One local landmark found just outside Kraków lies far beneath the earth's surface. The remarkable salt-mining town of Wieliczka has been in operation at least since the 13th century. Its nine levels reach a depth of over 984 feet (300 m). Visitors can take a fascinating 90-minute tour of the mines by elevator. They view underground chapels that house huge statues, altar rails and chandeliers carved from rock salt by the miners themselves. Other chambers contain a museum, a ballroom and even a tennis court for the miners. There is a more serious side to Wieliczka as well. Asthma patients find they can breath more easily in the salt-laden air of the mine. They are treated for their illness in a special sanatorium.

A more prosaic but vitally important part of Kraków's economy is Nowa Huta, literally "New Foundry," Poland's largest steel mill built by the Communists after World War II. The mill's 35,000 workers produce seven million tons of steel a year. The mill has brought both prosperity and problems to Kraków. Its poisonous fumes, along with those of the coal-fueled plants nearby, have created air pollution that is damaging the city's ancient buildings as well as posing a health hazard to its people.

Gdansk—Birthplace of Polish Freedom

Far to the north lies Poland's largest port city, Gdansk (pop. 465,000). Gdansk is one of Poland's newer cities, although it has a long and turbulent past. A Slavic settlement around the year 1000, Gdansk was taken over by the Teutonic Knights in 1308. The Poles and Knights struggled for control of the port for over a century. Poland finally won it in 1466. It became "Danzig," a Prussian port on the North Sea in 1793 during the second partition and remained so until 1919. It was returned to Poland in the Treaty of Versailles following World War I. The retaking of Gdansk by the Germans in 1939 sparked World War II. Danzig was returned to the Poles in May 1945 by the invading Russians. The Germans in Danzig were expelled and the city rechristened Gdansk. The city was famous again in 1980 when the trade union Solidarity was formed there by Lech Walesa and others.

Poland's most important port on the Baltic Sea, Gdansk has some of the largest shipyards in the world. It also is a center of the metallurgical and chemical industries, sawmilling, and brewing and distilling. Among Gdansk's historical buildings are the Gothic Church of St. Mary built in 1343 and one of the largest Protestant churches in the world.

Ancient Poznan and Gniezno

Older than Kraków, the city of Poznan (pop. 589,000) is the first fortified settlement built by the Polanie in the 800s and later home of the Piast kings. Like Gdansk, this city was taken over by the Prussians in 1792 and returned to Poland in 1919. Once a major trading center, Poznan revived its traditional spring fair day in 1922 as the International Trade Fair for capitalist and Communist countries to trade peacefully. Among Poznan's many historical landmarks are the Gold Chapel where the tombs of Mieszko I and his son Boleslaw the Brave reside.

Oldest of all Polish cities is Gniezno (pop. 70,000). It was the first capital of the Polish kingdom where kings were crowned until 1320 and the site where Christianity was first established in what is now Poland. Once a rural town of farmers, Gniezno now boasts a tannery, factories that produce shoes and other products, and engineering plants. It is home to a museum that includes relics of the first Piast kings, a beautiful 14th-century cathedral, and a modern auto race track.

Cultural Lublin and Wroclaw

Lovely Lublin (pop. 350,000) in southeastern Poland is home to five universities, including Catholic University, which was renamed the Maria Curie-Sklodowska University in 1944 in honor of Poland's greatest scientist. Lublin has played a critical role in Polish history. The legislative assemblies that united Poland and Lithuania in 1569 were held here. In 1918, Lublin was the seat of the temporary Polish Socialist government, and, in 1944, it was the seat of the provisional government that stood opposed to the Polish government-in-exile in London. Today Lublin is a manufacturing center as well as an educational one. Textiles, electrical products, agricultural machinery, and automobiles are made here.

Halfway between Poznan and Kraków in southwest Poland lies "The City of Bridges," Wroclaw (pop. 642,000). Some 84 bridges cross the Oder River in this quaint city, home to about 40,000 students at numerous colleges and the University of Wroclaw founded in 1811. In Wroclaw, also reside two of Poland's most distinguished theater companies—the Jerzy Grotowski Theatre Laboratory and the Henryk Tomaszewski Pantomime Theater. The city is a river port and a manufacturing center where textiles, machinery, iron goods, and railroad equipment are made.

Poland's cities have survived wars and invasions and have emerged triumphantly. They are living symbols of the perseverance and indomitable spirit of the Polish people.

NOTES

1. Katarzyna Wandycz, "The Polish Zoo," *Forbes*, May 25, 1992, p. 134.
2. Eric P. Kelly, *The Trumpeter of Krakow* (New York: Macmillan, 1966), pp. 18–19.
3. Jane Perlez, "Cracow Emerges from the Shadows," *The New York Times* (Sunday Travel section), July 18, 1993.

11

Present Problems and Future Solutions

Before looking at the problems facing this nation in transition, it might do well to look at what is right with Poland. The Polish economy in 1993 was the fastest growing in Europe, with the highest rate of growth in gross national product. Industrial production in the first half of 1993 rose 9.4 percent. Gross domestic production was up 3.9 percent in that same time period. In two years, inflation had fallen from over 100 percent to only 35 percent. Despite present hardships in the transitional phase from a planned economy to a market one, the Polish economy is in good shape and is growing stronger and more confident all the time.

Unlike some of its neighbors, such as the former Yugoslavia and Czechoslovakia, Poland is not troubled by ethnic divisiveness. Its generally well-educated, hard-working populace shares a common ancestry and traditions that will help it pull together for change, despite differences of opinion. Even Poland's geography, long a curse, may finally, in post-Communist Europe, prove a blessing. Its central location between a nonthreatening, reunited Germany and a Russia that has divested itself of its Soviet empire, may help it prosper both politically and economically.

This is the good news. Now for the problems and some possible solutions.

Unemployment

Despite tremendous gains in the economy, unemployment remains high in Poland where roughly one out of seven adults is out of work. At nearly 16 percent, its unemployment rate is the highest in Eastern Europe. About 38 percent of Poles also live below the poverty level. In contrast, the neighboring Czech Republic has very low unemployment, mainly because it has yet to make the tough decisions the Poles have made to reform their economy. The Czechs are still implementing the planned economy of the Communists and are only very gradually adopting to a free-market system.

Unemployment in Poland will surely drop as the new market economy fulfills its promise. In the meantime, the former Communist leadership must keep a delicate balance, meeting the needs of the people while not allowing the economy to slide back to the safety net of the Communist days.

The Business Management and Technological Gap

In many ways the Poles are in a better position to adapt to capitalism than their Eastern European neighbors. The Communists allowed more private businesses and farms to operate here than anywhere else behind the Iron Curtain. There are now over 1.6 million private businesses in the country and less than 8,000 state-owned companies left. A little over half of the work force is working in private business, accounting for half of the gross national product.

Despite these advantages, the Poles do not have the experience or skill to run their businesses as effectively as they could. Foreign investment and American corporations have been slow to move in and help out, not wanting to risk the failure that some companies, such as Gerber, have experienced. The Poles, like other Eastern Europeans, may have to make it largely on their own. One solution is to send top management abroad for training—another is to offer better training for students in business administration at home and work experience in Western-style companies. Those entrepreneurs who have succeeded, may be able to help others to find success in this new and sometimes frightening free marketplace. Finally, small businesses need to be able to borrow money more cheaply in order to grow. Current bank loans have exorbitant rates of interest, ranging from 40 to 60 percent per year. These need to be lowered substantially if small businesses are to survive and thrive.

The Long Shadow of Communism

As has been noted earlier, the reformed Communists of the Democratic Left Alliance now in power have created serious doubts about the sincerity of their commitment to reform. Events such as the dismissal of charges against two former Communist generals in the murder of a Solidarity priest, the nomination of former convicted spy Marion Zacharski to head the national intelligence agency, which might have jeopardized Polish-U.S. relations, and the passing of the Official State Secrets Act, have led many people to wonder if the Communists are planning a comeback in Poland.

While the threat to individual freedom cannot be ignored, the likelihood of a return to full-blown communism seems remote. If the Democratic Left Alliance wants to keep the reins of government, it will have to meet the demands of the people for democratic reform, politically as well as economically. If it does not, it may well find itself losing power in the next election.

But there is another, darker, aspect to Poland's Communist past. Decades of life under a system where all initiative was discouraged and the state cared, however poorly, for the needs of all citizens, have left the Poles crippled psychologically and spiritually.

As Halina Grzymala-Moszczynska, a professor at Jagiellonian University, notes, reliance on the Communist system and its sudden removal has created a condition of "learned helplessness":

This syndrome is more and more conspicuous in Poland. It is occasioned by the fear of losing one's job, combined with the deep conviction that nothing can be done to prevent this from happening. . . . After living under a command economy with virtually no unemployment, they are convinced that it is the state's obligation to supply citizens with jobs, not the citizens' role to look for jobs or to adapt to demands of the market.[1]

National Security

Surviving their enemies has always been a problem for Poland. While the collapse of communism has turned most of their enemies into friends, the Poles still are uncertain of the giant to the east—Russia. The economic and political turmoil that has enveloped post-Communist Russia in the past few years has the Poles and their neighbors concerned. Vladimir Zhirinovsky's Liberal Democrat Party, made up largely of nationalistic extremists, won nearly 25 percent of the vote in Russia's 1993 election, more than any other political party. By playing to the Russians' fear of foreigners and their desire to regain the status of a superpower, which was lost when the Soviet Union dissolved, Zhirinovsky has made himself a serious presidential contender when President Boris Yeltsin's term expires in 1996.

If Zhirinovsky, or another popular leader who appeals to the people's worst instincts, should come to power, will he move aggressively against Russia's nearest neighbor, Poland? Some Western observers claim this will not happen, that the Russians, regardless of who runs their country next, have too many problems at home to deal with to entertain retaking Eastern Europe. Nevertheless, the Poles, looking back on a long history of Russian aggression, are concerned.

In one poll taken in 1994, only 24 percent of those Poles questioned, thought of Russia as a "friendly state," while 81 percent expressed the desire for Poland to join the North Atlantic Treaty Organization (NATO).* Other Eastern European countries seeking the security of NATO member-

*An international group of 15 Western nations formed in 1949 to defend themselves collectively against aggression, particularly from the Soviet Bloc.

ship include Hungary, the Czech Republic, and Slovakia. The United States, a leader of NATO, at first seemed willing to allow these countries in. Then in early 1994, the United States withdrew the offer, not wanting to offend Russian nationalists who might be outraged by the West interfering in Eastern Europe. Instead, NATO offered Poland membership in what it called the "Partnership for Peace," a halfway measure that might one day lead to full membership in NATO. This was not acceptable to many Poles, including President Walesa. "There is no partnership yet," he said. "There is Russia, which threatens, the West, which is frightened, and us, in the middle."[2]

According to Andrzej Towpik, foreign ministry official in charge of relations with western defense institutions, the present threat from the East may be minimal, but cannot be ignored. "The security risks we are now facing are not risks to us from the East," he explained, "but the risks to stability in the East from the political, economic, and geographical transformation going on there. . . . You insure your car not because you think your neighbor will steal it tomorrow, but because you don't know what might happen to it in the future . . . Our fear is that we could be left aside and dismissed as insignificant."[3]

Crime

Since the fall of communism, crime has been on the upswing in Poland, as it has been in Russia and other Eastern European countries, where tight Soviet control once discouraged criminal activity. Crime has become highly organized, has the support of corrupt police, and is increasingly violent. Drug smuggling, prostitution, and murder for hire are now common in many cities.

Even Warsaw's venerable Old Town is not immune from the crime wave. In August 1994, shop owners in historic Market Square closed their doors in protest against organized crime's protection racket. Mob thugs have threatened violence if business owners do not pay the $500 to $7,000 a month for "protection."

"If the authorities allow this to happen only a few hundred meters [yards] from the Presidential Palace, what does that say about the rule of law in this country?"[4] complained restauranteur Roman Popowski.

Polish leaders are doing their best to cope with the situation and have sought the help of more experienced law enforcement agencies in the West. For example, the American Federal Bureau of Investigation (FBI) has opened an office in Warsaw to combat the infiltration of the Russian Mafia in Poland's capital.

The Environment

Poland's natural environment—it's air, water, land, and forests—are under serious assault from pollution. The threat to the environment is part of the grim legacy of communism and part of the bitter fruit of newly trans-planted capitalism. The steel furnaces built by the Soviets at Nowa Huta are hopelessly antiquated and continue to emit deadly clouds of carbon monoxide and sulfur dioxide that blanket the city of Kraków. Pollution control equipment installed by the U.S. Department of Energy has partially alleviated the problem, but until the furnaces are replaced, this modern dragon of Kraków will not be vanquished.

As Western prosperity has come to Poland, it has brought new problems with it. Capitalism has put over 5 million private cars on Poland's roadways, increasing air pollution and causing traffic jams in large cities. Emissions regulations for new cars are lax and unleaded gas is not yet mandatory. Western-style fast-food restaurants and other new businesses are turning Poles into greater consumers and the increase in disposable garbage, often sitting uncollected in cities for weeks, is alarming.

Some of Poland's environmental problems have their source outside the country's borders. The so-called Black Triangle, a plateau Poland shares with the Czech Republic and Germany, produces some of the worst acid rain in the world. The sulfur and soot from nearby coal-burning power plants mix with rain to destroy healthy forests. Over half of Poland's conifers and deciduous trees have lost over a quarter of their needles and leaves due to acid rain. As the trees die off, soil erosion will worsen, creating serious spring flooding.

Although more and more Poles are concerned about what pollution is doing to their country, the need for economic growth has so far out-stripped any concern for the environment. Until the economy fully recovers, Poland, like many other countries in Eastern Europe, will probably not turn its full attention to cleaning up the air, water, and land.

Education and Illiteracy

Although education is nearly universal, 70 percent of Poles have only a primary school education and only 6 out of 100 people have been to a university. According to research done at Poznan University, 30 percent of the population is functionally illiterate. Even more disturbing, nearly three-quarters of the people do not understand much of what they read and hear in the media. This is a bad constituency for a new democracy where people need to be prepared to make informed decisions based on

Poland's past and future come together on a park bench in Kraków, as an elderly man looks after his grandson. (Eric Miller/Impact Visuals)

A Polish Family in America

The great migration from Poland my grandparents were a part of did not begin in the 20th century, but goes back to the very beginnings of America. One of the first emigrant ships arriving in Jamestown in October 1608 included a group of Polish artisans, recruited to help establish the economic base of the tiny colony in present-day Virginia. They helped build a glassworks, which may have been the first factory in America.

Between 1900 and 1914 more Poles came to the United States than ever before. They were among the four largest groups of immigrants in the great wave of European immigration. Many of them settled in the new industrial cities of the Midwest—Milwaukee, Chicago, Detroit, and Cleveland—where they worked in factories, slaughterhouses, and mines.

Polish political refugees from communism began coming to America in the late 1940s up until the declaration of martial law in the early 1980s, when ordinary citizens were forbidden to leave Poland. Since the collapse of Communism in 1989, some Poles abroad have returned home, but many more have chosen to stay in their new homelands.

Not all the new immigrants have come for political reasons. Typical of this group are the Pierzak family of Stratford, Connecticut. Teresa Pierzak's grandparents came to America back in the late 1800s. They lived in Massachusetts, had two children, and then returned to Poland with their family shortly before the outbreak of World War I. The two oldest children returned to America to start new lives after the war, while Teresa's father,

the changing events going on around them. While the government is making some efforts to improve education, new funds will have to be found to make the educational system meet the needs of more of the population.

The Role of the Church

In the 40 years of a Communist-dominated Poland, the Roman Catholic Church played a dominant role in Polish life. It kept hope alive for millions of Poles. In post-Communist Poland, the church's attempts to control who was born in Poland, made the journey to America in the 1960s when he was 45.

Although life as an accountant for the government was steady and secure, her father was impressed by the good wages his sister was making in America. Teresa's mother refused to leave Poland, but a brother and sister later followed their father to America. The father returned home eventually, but the children stayed.

Teresa decided to come to America in 1976 when she was 23 years old. "It was a difficult decision," she explains. "When I first got here, I couldn't believe how much money I was paid. I thought to myself, 'How will I ever spend so much money?'"[5] Her first job was making screwdrivers in a factory. Later she became a nurse's aid, went back to school, and eventually became a registered nurse. Through mutual friends, she met her husband, Janusz, who had come to the United States in 1971.

Although the Pierzaks have adopted well to American life and their two children consider themselves Americans first, many of their friends are Polish and their social life is largely built around the Polish club they belong to. Janusz reads mostly Polish newspapers and magazines. The children take Polish dancing lessons. The family celebrates holidays with foods and traditions from their homeland.

Today, an estimated 7 to 15 million people of Polish descent live in the United States, more than any other country on earth outside of Poland. Chicago, the city with the largest Polish-American population—over a million—has more Poles than any city except Warsaw.

Polish society have been resented by millions of Catholic Poles. The church's efforts to push through legislation against abortion and contraceptives, and the efforts of priests to influence who their parishioners vote for, have caused the church to slip badly in public opinion polls. It has gone from being the most trusted institution in the country to fourth place, behind the army, the ombudsman,* and the police.

In January 1993, in an address to the entire assembly of Polish bishops, the pope warned against the church entering into politics in the new Poland and urged his fellow clergy to find a new role in their changing

---

*An official who investigates complaints against the government by private citizens.

society. He told them "the Church is not a political party nor is she identified with any political party; she is above them, open to all people of good will, and no political party can claim the right to represent her."[6] With the election of Bishop Tadeusz Pieronek, a relatively young clergyman who supports the pope's agenda, to the important position of general secretary of the Polish bishops' conference, the church may soon regain some of its lost prestige and influence.

Health

A naturally robust people, the Poles face serious health issues in the 21st century. Air pollution from widespread coal-burning plants has led to high rates of such respiratory diseases as emphysema, tuberculosis, and asthma. Birth defects and low birth rates are also a tragic result of growing air and water pollution. The government must increase expenditures on public health to combat these problems.

Other health problems are self-inflicted and reflect the high level of anxiety of a nation in transition. Both alcoholism and drug abuse are up. So is suicide, from 3,657 cases in all of 1989 to 3,000 cases in just the first half of 1993.

Ninety billion cigarettes are sold yearly in Poland, making Poles among the world's heaviest smokers. In 1992, 42 percent of all adults smoked, and 80,000 Poles die each year from the effects of smoking. The appearance of milder, filtered American-made cigarettes, may lower death rates, but will not solve this serious health problem. The government must take a stronger stand against smoking, as it has in the United States and other countries.

Perhaps the biggest problem facing Poland today is more psychological than political, geographical, or economic. There is a strange malaise that has overtaken the nation since the first heady days of freedom after communism's fall. Disillusionment over former heroes like Lech Walesa and the leaders of the Catholic Church, have made Poles, as a group, somewhat cautious and skeptical about the future. The election of former Communists to power shows that the Poles are not yet ready to close the door on the past for an unknown and untested future. This reaction is not as dangerous as it might be in Russia or some other Eastern European countries. The Poles, with a long tradition of democracy, do not have to overcome the czarist past of Russia, which has known little but autocratic rule in its history.

The autocrats who ruled Poland were usually invaders and conquerors. They may have conquered the Polish land, but never the soul of its people. It is this indomitable spirit that is Poland's best hope for the future, a future that promises to be perhaps this courageous and remarkable country's greatest golden age yet. In that sense, Poland is a model for other nations making the same difficult transition from communism to a more democratic system.

As one writer puts it, much more may hinge on Poland's successful transition to democracy than the fate of one nation.

> Poland is the vestibule [passageway] to the 21st century. If the current experiment in liberty succeeds in Poland, and if prosperity spreads throughout the land, then the prospects for liberty and prosperity in Belarus [a former republic of the Soviet Union] and in neighboring Ukraine improve considerably; and then so do those of Russia—and on eastward to China. Contrarily, if Poland fails, then the failure of the others is virtually foredoomed and the 21st century could become more tyrannous and bloody than the 20th.[7]

These are words worth heeding for all of us who value liberty and freedom.

NOTES

1. Halina Grzymala-Moszczynska, "Unlearning 'Learned Helplessness': The View from Poland," *Christian Century*, March 16, 1994, p. 281.
2. *The New York Times*, October 21, 1994.
3. *The New York Times*, September 30, 1994.
4. *The New York Times*, August 6, 1994.
5. Teresa Pierzak, personal interview with author.
6. George Weigel, "The Great Polish Experiment," *Commentary*, February 1994, p. 41.
7. Michael Novak, "Don't Abandon Us!" *Forbes*, January 17, 1994, p. 51.

Chronology

1793	The second partition is enacted by Prussia and Russia
1794	Koscuiszko's Uprising ends in defeat
1795	The Third Partition of Poland ends its existence as an independent state
1807	Napoleon creates the Duchy of Warsaw, briefly returning Poland to the map of Europe
1830	The first 19th-century uprising against the Russians begins in Warsaw
1863	The second Warsaw uprising ends in defeat for the Poles
1914	World War I begins; the Poles, under Josef Pilsudski, fight against the Russians on the Austrian side
1918	The Treaty of Versailles returns Poland to the status of an independent nation
1921	Russia returns some Polish territory under the Treaty of Riga
1923	Pilsudski resigns as premier
1926	Pilsudski becomes dictator in a bloodless military coup
1939	Poland is invaded by Germany and then Russia, setting off World War II
1943	Jews in the Warsaw Ghetto rise up against the Nazis in a month of fighting
1944	The second Warsaw uprising of World War II devastates the city as the Germans prepare to withdraw in the European war's last days
1945	Soviet Communists begin to take over the government of Poland
1948	The Soviets clamp down; Communist Party leader Wladyslaw Gomulka is forced to resign
1952	Stefan Cardinal Wyszynski is imprisoned
1956	Antigovernment demonstrations and riots in Poznan and other cities lead to some reforms and the return of Gomulka to power

| 1968 | Student strikes and protests against the government at the University of Warsaw and elsewhere lead to the firing of numerous teachers, many of whom leave the country |

1970

December 15	On "Bloody Tuesday," 55 workers in Gdansk are killed by police in "bread riots" that lead to the burning of the city's Communist Party headquarters
December 20	Edward Gierek replaces Gomulka as Communist Party leader
1978	Karol Cardinal Wojtyla, archbishop of Kraków is elected pope of the Roman Catholic Church and becomes John Paul II

1980

August	An organization of trade unions is recognized by the government and workers win the right to strike and have unions
September	Gierek is replaced as party leader by Stanislaw Kania
December	Rural Solidarity, a trade organization for farmers, is founded in Warsaw

1981

September	Solidarity's first national Congress of Delegates convenes in Gdansk
October	Kania is replaced by General Wojciech Jaruzelski
November	After some foot dragging, the government recognizes Solidarity
December 13	Jaruzelski declares martial law and Solidarity's activities are suspended

1982

October   Solidarity is officially outlawed; Lech Walesa
                            wins the Nobel Peace Prize

1983

June   Pope John Paul II visits Poland for the third time
                            and acts as a mediator between Solidarity and
                            the government

1984

October   Father Jerzy Popieluszki, a Solidarity priest, is
                            murdered by secret police, setting off a national
                            protest

1985   Mikhail Gorbachev becomes the new leader of the
                            Soviet Union and soon begins far-reaching reforms

1987   Price increases of up to 100 percent on goods
                            and services are announced

1989

February   Roundtable discussions begin between the gov-
                            ernment and Solidarity leaders

April   The two sides sign accords legalizing Solidarity
                            and preparing the way for free elections

June 4   In the first free elections since the end of World
                            War II, Solidarity wins 99 of 100 seats in the new
                            senate

July 4   The new Polish parliament convenes

November   Lech Walesa visits the United States and ad-
                            dresses a joint meeting of Congress

1990

January   The Communist Party of Poland votes to dis-
                            band itself; Prime Minister Tadeusz Mazowiecki
                            declares a program of radical economic reform

September	Jaruzelski resigns as president and new presidential elections are scheduled
December	Lech Walesa becomes the first popularly elected president in 50 years

1991

October	The first fully free parliamentary election brings 29 political parties into parliament

1992

June	Walesa's first coalition government falls apart. Hanna Suchocka becomes the first female prime minister in Eastern Europe in the 20th century as her Democratic Union Party wins in new elections

1993

April	The lower house approves a privatization plan for state-owned industry
September	The Democratic Left Alliance, made up of former Communists, ousts the Democratic Union from power
October	Waldemar Pawlak, leader of the Polish Peasant Party, becomes the sixth prime minister since the fall of communism

1994

January	NATO announces that Poland and other Eastern European countries are invited to be part of its newly formed "Partnership for Peace"
June	The first military exercises of 13 countries representing "Partnership for Peace" are held in Poland

August

Two Polish generals are acquitted of involvement in the murder of Father Popieluszki over the protests of the people

September

The Official State Secrets Act, a blow for many to democratic reforms, passes in the lower house of parliament

1995

February

Jozef Oleksy, a senior member of the Democratic Left Alliance, becomes prime minister, replacing Pawlak

Further Reading

Nonfiction Books

Ascherson, Neal. *The Struggles for Poland.* New York: Random House, 1987. A concise adult history of Poland in the 20th century through the mid-1980s.

Davies, Norman. *God's Playground: A History of Poland.* Vols. I and II. New York: Columbia University Press, 1982. A monumental study of Polish history from its beginnings to the last decade of communism. Written for adults.

Donica, Ewa, and Tim Sharman. *We Live in Poland.* New York: Bookwright Press, 1985. Part of a fascinating young adult series that views Poland through interviews with individuals in representative roles and careers.

Greene, Carol. *Poland.* Chicago: Children's Press, 1983. An excellent well-illustrated introduction for young adults to Polish history and culture, part of the "Enchantment of the World" series.

Gwertzman, Bernard, and Michael T. Kaufman, eds. *The Collapse of Communism.* New York: Times Books, 1990. A blow-by-blow chronological account from the pages of the *New York Times* of events in Poland, the Soviet Union, and other countries in Eastern Europe during the critical years 1989–1990.

Madison, Arnold. *Polish Greats.* New York: David McKay Co., 1980. Short biographies of such famous Poles as Copernicus, Koscuiszko, Chopin, and Pope John Paul. Young adult.

Michener, James. *Pilgrimage: A Memoir of Poland and Rome.* Emmaus, Pa.: Rodale Press, 1990. Thoughts and observations of this leading American novelist during a 1988 trip to Poland and the Vatican to visit with Pope John Paul.

Pfeiffer, Christine. *Poland—Land of Freedom Fighters.* Minneapolis, Minn.: Dillon Press, 1984. Another fairly comprehensive survey of Poland before communism's fall, for young adults.

Weschler, Lawrence. *Solidarity: Poland in the Season of Its Passion.* New York: Simon & Schuster, 1982. A detailed inside look at the rise of Solidarity in the earth-shaking year 1981, ending with the establishment of martial law.

Fiction Books

Borowski, Tadeusz. *This Way for the Gas, Ladies and Gentlemen.* New York: Penguin, 1976. Gripping stories about everyday life in the Polish concentration camps of World War II by a Polish writer who lived through the nightmare.

Kelly, Eric P. *The Trumpeter of Krakow.* New York: Macmillan, 1966. A Newbery Award–winning novel for young adults about a family's progress in 15th-century Kraków. An outstanding historical novel first published in 1928.

Michener, James. *Poland.* New York: Fawcett Crest, 1984. An epic journey through Polish history tracing the fortunes of three families by an American master of the historical novel.

Mrozek, Slawomir. *The Elephant.* New York: Grove Press, 1965. Short, satirical, fablelike stories by a leading contemporary Polish writer that mock the bureaucratic soullessness of the Communist government and the people living under it.

Sienkiewicz, Henryk. *With Fire and Sword.* New York: Hippocrene Books, 1991. The last volume in this Nobel Prize–winning Polish novelist's trilogy about turbulent 17th-century Poland.

Index

Entries are filed letter by letter. *Italic* page references indicate illustrations and captions. Roman numerals and page references followed by *m* indicate maps. Locators followed by *c* indicate chronology.